Politics of the Ordinary

Cover from a painting by the German Jewish painter Felix Nussbaum (1904-1944). Site of the Museum of his work: http://www.osnabrueck.de/werkverzeichnis/. Nussbaum has—while firmly rooted in the European tradition of modern art—given the atrocities of Nazism a face. We honor his life and work by pointing at his artwork on the covers of this series *Ethics of Care*.

Felix Nussbaum
Stilleben mit Regenschirm, um 1939, WV nr. 361
Oil on canvas, 88 × 71 cm
Private collection

Permanent loan from the Niedersächsischen Sparkassenstiftung

Ethics of Care
Volume 11

Politics of the Ordinary
Care, Ethics, and Forms of Life

Sandra Laugier

PEETERS
Leuven – Paris – Bristol, CT
2020

A catalogue record for this book is available from the Library of Congress.

ISBN 978-90-429-4249-3
eISBN 978-90-429-4250-9
D/2020/0602/103

Table of Contents

Acknowledgments VII

Introduction: Care and Life 1

I Politics of Vulnerability 9
II Ethics and What Matters 23
III Care and Ordinary Language Philosophy 39
IV Responsibility for Ordinary Others 55
V Attention, Security, and the Transformation of Ethics 65
VI Care as Subversion 77

Bibliography 89

Acknowledgments

The author and the editor wish to thank Ms. Daniela Ginsburg for translating the original text of this book (French-English) and Ms Dr. Kareni Bannister, Oxford, for the final revisions and check-up.

Our heartfelt thanks to Ms. Cécile Gagnon, Université Laval, Canada, for her supportive editing work.

We thank Panthéon Sorbonne University (Paris), the University of Humanistic Studies (Utrecht, the Netherlands) and the Foundation Critical Ethics of care (Utrecht) for their valuable financial support.

This book would not exist without the exchanges, and the long term solidarity, with Carol Gilligan, Fabienne Brugère, Pascale Molinier, Patricia Paperman.

It also owes a lot to the support and care of Frans Vosman.

I am deeply grateful to him.

Introduction: Care and Life

To Frans Vosman

> As for adopting the ways which the State has provided for remedying the evil, I know not of such ways. They take too much time, and a man's life will be gone. I have other affairs to attend to. I came into this world, not chiefly to make this a good place to live in, but to live in it, be it good or bad. (Thoreau, *Civil Disobedience*)

The ordinary has been variously denied, undervalued, or neglected—not taken into account—in theoretical thought. Such negligence, I propose, has to do with widespread contempt for ordinary life inasmuch as it is domestic and female. The disdain stems from the gendered hierarchy of objects deemed worthy of intellectual research. One important aspect of ordinary language philosophy, as I see it, is its capacity to call our attention to human expressiveness as embodied in women's voices. Ordinary language philosophy (OLP) thus provides the basis for a redefinition of ethics as attention to ordinary life, and care for moral expression.

The idea of an ethics formulated in a "different voice"—a woman's voice—follows from these explorations of OLP, with the further incorporation of Carol Gilligan's approach as a developmental psychologist. Care is at once a practical response to specific needs and a sensitivity to the ordinary details of human life that *matter*. Hence, care is a concrete matter that ensures maintenance (for example, as conversation and conservation) and continuity of the human world and form of life. This is nothing less than a paradigm shift in ethics, with a reorientation toward vulnerability and a shift from the "just" to the "important." Measuring the importance of care for human life requires first acknowledging the truth that we arrived at in the last chapter, following Austin: that human life forms are fundamentally vulnerable, subject to failure, and even defined by the possibility of error. To pay attention to ordinary life is to become aware of its vulnerability—it is constantly threatening to dissolve or else to reveal itself to have been unreal all along, a mere fantasy.

Human vulnerability is the "original condition" of the need for care—what needs to be taken care of and cared about. I want to add here a connection between security/safety, vulnerability (Laugier 2016ab), and care, of which I became aware when I encountered the reality of the Fukushima human disaster. The situation in post-catastrophic Japan raises the issue of human security, in a very basic way (Laugier 2013b).

Various humanitarian programs that promote security, and human security, aim to give a list of positive items that would define security, as preservation of basic vital interests: interests related to health, environment, body, sexuality, membership in a political community, work, gender, sexuality. The concept of security thus provides a reformulation of the capability approach, introduced by authors such as Amartya Sen and Martha Nussbaum. (It is not an accident that Sen served as President of the Commission of Human Security of UN.) But Sen himself reminds us, in "Human Security Now" (2003), that the basic reality is *insecurity*: what he calls "the intense problem of human insecurity". Our problem is, more, insecurity, or precariousness, than security. This is why the paradigm of care is so powerful, after having been neglected since the second wave of feminism. Precariousness (not related etymologically to care!) and vulnerability are conditions of the human life form today.

It is not about living a "good" life, but just about living a life. This notion of *human life* is connected to Wittgenstein's idea of a form of life/life form (a form taken by life, as Cavell, 1979 and Das, 2007 say), which also defines a texture of life. "Texture" thus refers to an unstable reality that cannot be fixed by concepts, or by determinate particular objects, but only by the recognition of gestures, manners, details and styles. We can connect the ethics of care to the idea of the vulnerability of the human and of life. Cavell, Diamond, and Das work to connect the very idea of the vulnerability of the human to a vulnerability of our life form(s). *Lebensformen* in Wittgenstein, Cavell stresses, should be translated not by the phrase forms of life, but life forms (1979). This idea of a life form is connected, for Cavell and Das, to Wittgenstein's anthropological sensitivity, to his attention to everyday language forms, as being both obvious and strange, foreign, and vulnerable (Das 2007). The uncanniness of the ordinary, for Cavell, is thus not resolved in the return to everyday life and words; the human, or life, is not a given; it is defined by the permanent threat of denial of the human, of dehumanization or even "devitalization," loss of form of life.

Attention to what Veena Das calls *the everyday life of the human* (2007) is the first step of caring: care is attention, and the ethics of care calls our attention to phenomena commonly unseen, but which stand right before our eyes. Das (2007) and Cavell (1979) draw our attention to the ordinary by making us attentive to human expressiveness. This is attention to what is right before our eyes (the visible) and to human capacities for expression as connected to capacities for suffering. The idea of the vulnerable is connected to the idea of expression and to the human body as carrying expression, fated to expressivity but also refusing it ("us victims of expression," says Emerson (1977).

The perspective of *care*, by calling our attention to our general situation of dependence, is thus indissociably political and ethical; it develops an analysis of social relations organized around dependence and vulnerability—blind spots of the ethics of justice. In response to the "original position" described by Rawls (1971), the perspective of *care* would tend to set this "original condition" of vulnerability as the anchor point of moral and political thought. Not a position on which to build an ideal theory or set principles, but the mere fact of vulnerability that appears in "the difficulty of reality." This is something that is obvious in the contexts *Life and Words* (2007; see also Laugier 2015) accounts for, when violence destroys the everyday and the sense of life as defining the human.

In Swapan's story, as told by Das in *Affliction* (2015), care is care for the preservation of form of life, life being threatened by madness. The threat to normality (normal family life) becomes a threat to reality itself. We can use here what Goffman says, in "The

Insanity of Place" (1969), about the unreality of life as it is remembered (as a dream) after the crisis created by the occurrence of madness in a family. But this unreality appears in ordinary incidents.

> Whether crucial or picayune, all encounters present occasions when the individual can become spontaneously involved in the proceedings and derive from this a firm sense of reality. When an incident occurs and spontaneous involvement is threatened, then reality is threatened.... The minute social system that is brought into being with each encounter will be disorganized, and the participants will feel unruled, unreal, and anomic. (Goffman, 2005, p. 135)

Care is "a perspective from which to think about human life," Tronto reminds us. It is also a political guideline. Not only, as Tronto has shown in *Moral Boundaries*, to set a new agenda for public policies and moral priorities. The critical import of such questions is huge and makes *care* an issue of citizenship and humanity. But also, now, as a new definition of citizenship as humanity and bounds of care.

For Tronto, we should think of care as a ground for conferring citizenship: this is what she means by "care is the work of citizens" (1993, 2005). In a world in which we took the centrality of care more seriously, we would define citizens as people engaged in relationships of care with one another. *Citizens* equates with *people engaged in relations of care with one another*. If we adopt such a seemingly modest definition of citizenship, it would require a radical rethinking of political values.

The issue of care today is made more urgent by the crisis of care and the global injustice of global poverty: by focusing on and valuing care in the North, we insulate people in the North from the harm their actions inflict upon others. Ordinary citizens in the Anglo-American world, says Tronto, lack determinate knowledge about their complicity in global poverty. So there is a strong connection between care and global justice, a connection that seems to hollow out the classical care/justice debate, for only the care perspective enables us to really take care of the problem of global injustice. The main inequalities, today, are in the area of care.

> Women are the world's primary, and usually only, care-givers for people in a condition of extreme dependency: Young children, the elderly, and those whose physical or mental handicaps make them incapable of the relative (and often temporary) independence that characterizes so-called 'normal' human lives. Women perform this crucial work, often, without pay and without recognition that it is work. At the same time, the fact that they need to spend long hours caring for the physical needs of others makes it more difficult for them to do what they want to do in other areas of life, including employment, citizenship, play and self-expression. (Nussbaum, 2000b, p. 222)

Nussbaum adds that women lack essential support for leading lives that are fully human. And even when they live in a constitutional democracy such as India, where they are equals in theory, they are second-class citizens in reality. So, issues of care and insecurity are the most urgent issues of justice: by articulating Care and Citizenship, we see that what is at issue is not the warranting of universal (and unavailable) human rights, or (in the capabilities approach) the possibility of living a full life, or at least to lead a safe human life. What is at issue is political citizenship in a world where it is denied to a majority of humans, hence denied humanity. Citizenship signifies political membership, having a voice in your history. But today citizenship has become an exclusionary practice (and this is the source of many mobilizations and revolts) even, and most prominently, in democracies. Citizenship is determined by the people who live in a nation state that sets the rules for membership.

> Like a private club that understands the value of its exclusionary rules for inclusion, citizenship can function as a kind of barrier that reflects and protects the political power of those who are already insiders. Citizenship is not always determined, then, by what is moral and just. The question of citizenship is quintessentially a political question, and political questions call for political solutions. (Tronto, in Marilyn Friedman (ed.), 2005)

Questions about citizenship are also close to care issues because they are always local questions. They concern the decisions about membership that are made by the closed circle of those who are already members. "Discussions about citizenship must always then be local and political, and cannot only be made in universal and moral terms" (Tronto, 2005, p. 144). Models of citizenship define the boundaries between public and private life and determine which activities, attitudes, possessions, etc., are to be considered worthy in any given state. In previous historical eras, property or arms were conditions of citizenship. Through inclusion and exclusion of some people, citizenship reflects winners and losers in the political game with the highest stakes.

Societies conceive of citizens in terms of the contributions they make to society. Definitions of citizenship change when there is a political movement by non-citizens, who consider their contribution important, one which sufficiently threatens existing members into changing their definitions of citizenship. But the important issue here is to define citizenship by vulnerability, by needs instead of "contribution." Here radical insecurity can become the basis of a new, inclusive definition of citizenship, a citizenship not defined (just as security) by the protection of a particular state (just as human security has been defined in terms of claim to security that belongs primarily to individuals and societies, and only secondarily to States) but by a protection of the human as such. As Amartya Sen says in defense of his capabilities approach for thinking Human Security:

> We are asking the world community to look particularly at the interconnections that have to be taken into account in developing a fuller and more integrated approach to the insecurities that plague the lives of so much of humanity. We believe that the effectiveness of our battle against human insecurity requires collaboration at different levels. First of all, focusing on the concern with vulnerability and insecurity can itself be valuable in bringing an important perspective to the *attention* of the world. (Sen 2003)

The concept of human security seems to indicate both the need of being protected (from above) and the need of being enabled (from below, or horizontally) to pursue one's own vital interests: interests related to health, environment, body, membership in a community, work, and so on. But it is also a democratic challenge.

The concept of human security provides a reformulation and enactment of the capability approach. It harks back, therefore, to this long history of normative claims to protection and promotion of the vital interests of singular human beings. But chiefly, as appears in Sen's *The Idea of Justice* (2009), the point of view of human security is a bottom-up normative (philosophical, political, social) conception. A bottom-up conception reconstructs from below the ordinary demands of justice, welfare, interests, etc., rather than accounting for such demands from above—that is, from a description of perfect institutions which is applied only in later stages to concrete circumstances. So, the Human Security approach can contribute to the heterodox view of ethics we are calling for, by appealing to the bottom-up approach, which emphasizes the role of social and individual grounds rather than the outlining of institutions; and by appealing to the bottom-up perspective to the dimension of human needs, vulnerabilities, necessities, etc. The concept of Human Security is essential to a development of bottom-up normative perspectives, bottom being human vulnerability.

Bottom-up perspectives do not derive normative criteria from above, through a description of a society perfectly governed by morally justified principles and institutions: normative criteria are derived, instead, from an examination of specific situations which appear, from different points of view, unjust or immoral or simply unbearable. Following Sen's account in *The Idea of Justice*, we need to find alternatives to transcendental institutionalism—the approach that confines the issue of justice within the description of institutions and principles, thus obscuring the description of concrete societies and actual conducts, circumstances and situations. As Sen shows, when it comes to these critical and reflexive practices, a theory developed from the top down is neither necessary nor sufficient: ordinary practices do not require a perfect theory.

Adopting a bottom-up model based on vulnerability can shed light on the importance of political relations that are not perceivable within a top-down approach, or with classical and conformist bottom-top approaches of liberal democracies. Political relations must be left open to the questioning of a wide range of human relations, such as: the various forms of care, trust, familiarity, and community that are generated in globalized societies, where people who are and remain strangers are living together, and where one can encounter people in further circles. These relations of trust and reliance among strangers are vital to the creation of a texture of security. In order to build up a safer society we need therefore to attend to those horizontal networks of relations and communities that, while not being strictly speaking political, have an expressive political relevance through the acknowledgement of vulnerability or precariousness.

The notion of vulnerability indicates contexts of ordinary life, in which human beings find their needs, interests, and fragilities totally exposed. These contexts are governed by relations that cannot be made even perceptible, visible, through the orthodox or liberal concepts of ethics (justice, impartiality, catalogue of duties, rational choice, etc.). The disconnection of citizenship and possession of rights in favor of a citizenship based on vulnerability and networks of care is probably the first challenge, in times of disaster, for a care ethics, made more urgent both by the fragilization and the plasticity of human forms of life.

1 Politics of Vulnerability

By proposing to valorize moral values primarily defined as "feminine"—caring, attention to others, solicitude—the ethics of *care* has contributed to modifying a dominant conception of ethics, and has changed deeply the way we look at ethics, or conceive of what ethics should look like. It has introduced ethical stakes into politics, weakening, through its critique of theories of justice, the seemingly obvious link between an ethics of justice and political liberalism. But an important aspect is perhaps to be found in the kinds of resistance that ethics of care encounters: theoretical objections to ethics of *care* are connected with a frequent rejection of the demand—immediately seen to be essentialist—for a specifically *feminine* ethics. However, *care* corresponds to a quite ordinary reality: the fact that people look after one another, take care of one another, and thus are attentive to the functioning (or the commerce) of the world, which depends on this kind of care.

Ethics of *care* affirms the importance of care and attention given to others, in particular to those whose lives and wellbeing depend on directed and constant attention. Ethics of care draws our attention to the ordinary, to what we are unable to see precisely because it is right before our eyes. So before being a feminine ethics, it is an ethics that gives a voice to humans who are undervalued precisely because they accomplish unnoticed, invisible tasks, and take care of basic needs.

This ethics arises in response to historical conditions that have favored a division of moral labor such that activities of care have been socially and morally devalorized. The assignment of women to the domestic sphere has reinforced the exclusion of these activities and preoccupations from the moral domain and the public sphere, reducing them to the rank of private sentiments devoid of moral and political import. The perspectives of *care* carry with them a fundamental claim concerning the importance of care for human life, for the relations that organize it, and the social and moral position of care-givers. (Kittay and Feder, 2002). Recognizing this means recognizing that dependence and vulnerability are traits of a condition common to all, not of a special category of the "vulnerable." This sort of "ordinary" realism (in the sense of "realistic," proposed by Diamond, 1991) is largely absent from the majority of social and moral theories, which tend to reduce the activities and preoccupations of *care* to a concern for the weak on the part of selfless mothers, and nothing more than a sentimental fact. Hence the importance of acknowledging the first principle of the ethics of care: *the person is vulnerable*. It is an anthropological teaching, both ordinary and tragic. This is how Cavell defines the everyday, and the anthropological tonality of any approach to everyday life:

> The intersection of the familiar and the strange is an experience of the uncanny (…)
> What I call Wittgenstein's anthropological perspective is one puzzled in principle by anything human beings say and do, hence perhaps, at a moment, by nothing. (Preface of Cavell in Das, 2007, p. x)

The ethics of care leads us to a completely different view of the aim of ethics, by drawing our attention to ordinary and usually unseen details of our lives. The philosophical craving for generality is "contempt for the particular case"; moral perception is care for the particular. In "Vision and Choice in Morality" (1997), Iris Murdoch writes of the importance of attention in morality. (This is one initial manner in which we may express *care*: to pay attention to, to be attentive.) *Attention* is part of the ethical meaning of *care*: one must pay attention to these details of life that we neglect.

Attention, care, are part of a new understanding of human experience as singular. As Cavell says:

> I think of this as checking one's experience—which entails consulting one's experience, subjecting it to examination, as well as momentarily stopping, turning yourself away from whatever your preoccupation and turning your experience away from its expected, habitual track, to find its own track: coming to attention. (Cavell, 1981, p. 12)

Care is defined on the basis of this specific attention to the importance of things and moments, to its inherent concealment. This fragility of the real and of experience, to speak in Goffman's idiom (1987), is characteristic of ordinary experience, which is "structurally vulnerable" since its sense is never *given*. The reorientation of morality toward importance and its connection to the structural vulnerability of experience could define the ethics of *care*. The notion of *care* is indissociable from a whole cluster of terms that comprise a language game of the particular: attention, care, importance, significance, to count. It is in the use of language (choice of words, style of expression and conversation) that a person's moral vision, his or her *texture of being*, is intimately developed and openly shown. This texture has little to do with choices and moral arguments but instead with what matters and gives expression to the differences between singulars.

> We cannot see the moral interest of literature unless we recognize gestures, manners, habits, turns of speech, turns of thought, styles of face as morally expressive. The intelligent description of such things is part of the intelligent, the sharp-eyed, description of life, of what matters, makes differences, in human lives. (Diamond, 1991, p. 375)

A form of life, from the point of view of ethics, is defined by perception—attention to moral textures or motifs (described by Diamond and Nussbaum (in Laugier 2006) in their essays on Henry James). These motifs are perceived to be "morally expressive." Literature is a privileged site of moral perception, through its creation of a background that makes moral perception possible, by allowing important (significant) differences to appear. An example is J. M. Coetzee: to read what he writes in *Disgrace* about animals makes you see them differently, how they matter in our moral world.

> Justification, in ethics as anywhere else, goes on within lives we share with others, but what we may count in that life is not laid down in advance. The force of what we are able to say depends on its relation to the life of the words we use, the place of those words in our lives. (Diamond, 1991, p. 27)

Martha Nussbaum (1990) defines ethical competence in terms of an active and fine-tuned perception (in contrast to the ability to judge, make arguments, and choose). For her, morality is a matter of perception and attention, and not one of argument. One possible objection to her approach would be that one then returns to a caricatural opposition between sentiment and reason. Novels teach us to regard moral life as "the scene of adventure and improvisation," which transforms the idea we have of moral *agency* and makes visible to us "the values in moral improvisation" (Diamond, 1991 p. 316). Within such an approach, *care* is at the root of ethics, rather than a subordinate or marginal element of it. Moral learning defines ethics as attention to the real and to others. It is initiation into a form of life and a sensible training based on exemplarity. Morality (and politics) thus concerns our ability to read and assess moral expression. This ability is not purely affective; it is *conceptual* and *linguistic*—it is our ability to make good use of words, to use them in new contexts, to respond/react correctly.

As Charles Taylor has said, ability for moral expression is rooted in a malleable form of life, vulnerable to our good and bad uses of language. It is the form of life (in the natural sense, as social) that determines the (ethical) structure of expression, which inversely reworks it and gives it form.

> This structure can only be put to work against a background that we can never completely dominate, for we remodel it endlessly, without dominating it and without having an overlooking view. (Taylor, 1985)

The relationship to the other, the type of interest and care that we have for others, the importance we give them, exist only in their singular and public expression. What Cavell describes in a skeptical mode is described by Taylor in a more "hermeneutic" mode, but both lead to moral questioning on the basis of mutual expression, of the constitution of style and the apprenticeship of attention to the expressions of others: "Human expression, the human figure, to be understood, must be *read*" (Cavell, 1979, p. 363). This reading of expression, this sensibility to meaning, which makes *responding* possible, is the product of attention and of *care*.

We must modify and enlarge our sense of rationality based on the notion of ethical rationality, without thereby rejecting all form of argumentation or returning to the conformism of founding ethics in practice. The focus, a result of the influence of Kant and Rawls, on moral notions such as duty or choice leaves out essential ordinary moral questioning, and has been insufficient for reflecting on the ordinary moral problems that *care* poses. As Diamond remarks, someone who is perfectly rigorous and moral may be petty or stingy, and this unlovable (in the strong sense) trait is something that could, instead of being considered a vague, non-ethical, psychological concept, form an integral part of moral reflection. Baier suggests that we focus on a quality such as *gentleness*, which can only be treated in descriptive and normative terms and which "resists analysis in terms of rules" (Baier, 1985, p. 219), since this quality is a response appropriate to the other, *according to circumstance*: it necessitates an experimental attitude, sensibility to the situation, and the ability to improvise, to "move on to something else" when faced with certain reactions. According to Baier, the legalist paradigm perverts moral reflection:

> Those who object to analytic methods most often reject not only the comparison of philosophical thought to mathematical computation, but also the legalist paradigm, the tyranny of the argument. (Baier, 1985, p. 241)

Baier, like Murdoch, criticizes the idea that moral philosophy can be reduced to questions of obligation and choice—as if a moral problem, since it can be formulated in these terms, can also be treated thus. Baier takes up I. Hacking's (1984) observations on moral philosophy's obsession with the model of game theory. For Baier, this is a masculine syndrome ("a big boy's game, and a pretty silly one too"). Certainly, ordinary moral life is full of decisions. But what leads up to decisions is just as much the work of improvisation as the work of reasoning or the application of principles. Tronto puts it beautifully:

> Care requires justice, but it also requires that we think of justice in concrete cases and circumstances, not just as a general set of principles that are left to courts, politicians, or philosophers, to apply. (Tronto, 1993, p. 14)

It is sometimes feared (Ogien, 1998, 2004) that the anti-theoretic and "ordinary" approach could lead to a new and perverse form of foundationalism and conservatism, encouraging us to rely on customs and traditions rather than on argued principles. Murdoch has argued very well against this argumentative neutrality of morality: the very idea of neutrality is itself liberal, and is ideologically situated within liberalism. Cavell's somewhat different response to this fear bears on the difficulty of saying who this *we* is—what is the custom or tradition on which we would rely. The essential question concerning morality is perhaps that of the point of departure, of the given. This specific relation to our "ordinary claims to knowledge," to ordinary moral authority, is, according to Cavell, an essential element for defining moral life and the nature of our moral agreement. My agreement or my belonging to *this or that* form of life, social or moral, is not given. The background is not *a priori* and can be modified by practice itself. The form of this acceptance, the limits and scales of our agreement, are not knowable *a priori*, "no more than one can *a priori* know the scope or scale of a word" (Cavell, 1989, p. 44).

> There is a pervasive and systematic background of agreements among us, which we had not realized, or had not known we realize. Wittgenstein sometimes calls them conventions, sometimes rules… The agreement we act upon he calls 'agreement in judgments' (§242), and he speaks of our ability to use language as depending upon agreement in 'forms of life' (§241). But forms of life, he says, are exactly what have to be 'accepted'; they are 'given'. (Cavell, 1979, p. 30)[1]

[1] See Laugier, 2015, 2018

That we agree in language means that language—our form of life—produces our understanding of one another just as much as it itself is a product of agreement. Language is natural to us in this sense; the idea of convention is there to at once ape and disguise this necessity. "Beneath the tyranny of convention, there is the tyranny of nature." Cavell writes (1979, p. 46). At this point, the criticism mounted by Cavell of the usual interpretations of "form of life" becomes relevant. Cavell opposes these interpretations by his use of the translation *life form* rather than *form* of life. What is given is our form of life. What leads us to want to violate our agreements, our criteria, is the refusal of this given, of this form of life in not only its social but also its biological dimension. It is on this second (vertical) aspect of form of life that Cavell is insisting, while at the same time recognizing the importance of the first (horizontal) dimension, i.e., social agreement. What discussions of the first sense (that of conventionalism) have obscured is the strength for Wittgenstein of the natural and biological sense of form of life, which he picks out in evoking "natural reactions" and "the natural history of humanity." What is given in forms of life is not only social structures and various cultural habits, but everything that can be seen in "the specific strength and dimensions of the human body, the senses, the human voice" and everything that makes it the case that, just as doves, in Kant's phrase, need air to fly, so we, in Wittgenstein's phrase, need friction to walk (*Philosophical Investigations*, §107).

It is a wonderful step towards understanding the abutment of language and the world when we see it to be a matter of convention. But this idea, like every other, endangers as it releases the imagination. For some will then suppose that a private meaning is not more arbitrary than one arrived at publicly, and that since language inevitably changes, there is no reason not to change it arbitrarily. Here we need to remind ourselves that ordinary language is natural language, and that its changing is natural.

Let us turn to an example that Diamond gives, in which Peter Singer declares himself in favor of the defense of animals:

> What I mean by 'stupid or insensitive or crazy' may be brought out by a single word, the word 'even' in this quotation: 'We have seen that the experimenter reveals a bias in favor of his own species whenever he carries out an experiment on a non-human for a purpose that he would not think justified him in using a human being, even a retarded human being.' (Diamond, 1991, p. 23)

What does not work in such an argument is not the argument itself, but the use of this terrifying word "even": the absence of *care*. When Diamond affirms that moral philosophy has become blind and insensitive, she means insensitive to the human specificity of moral questioning and to ordinary moral life. This does not mean that the morality she wishes to promote would be indifferent to exceptional situations, which may in fact be situations of choice, but rather, that the tragedy of great decisions is in a certain way inherent to and contained within the ordinary; our everyday problems require the same attention and care. It is this dimension of tragedy that separates an ordinary ethics from theories of consensus and community, from an alleged common sense to which one has easy recourse in justifying conformist positions. What matters, in moral perception, is not agreement and harmony but the perception of contrasts, distances, differences and their expression. It is that moment in which there is a "loss of concepts," when something doesn't work any more...

> A sensibility to the conceptual world in which someone's remarks are situated is a moment of human sensibility to words...I am now interested in our ability to recognize the moment in which someone's words show, or seem to show, a way of leaving the common conceptual world. (Diamond, 1988, pp. 273–4)

On Diamond's account here, there is not an opposition between sensibility and understanding, but rather, a sensibility to a form of a *conceptual life*. This is what explains the "sensible" reactions we have to ideas. There is no need to separate argument and sentiment in ethics, as Nussbaum sometimes does and as certain formulations of *care* risk implying. It is rather the sensible character of concepts and the perceptive character of conceptual activity which are at work:

they allow for *the* clear vision of conceptual contrasts and distances (as, for example, when one hears someone speaking and without necessarily being able to offer arguments against what he or she is saying, *knows* that it is somehow not right at all). To give *care* its place, one must give it the greatest place, and consider that morality as a whole must become sensible—a "sensibility which would encompass the totality of the spirit." This question—of expression and experience, of when and how to *trust one's experience*, of finding the validity proper to the particular—goes beyond the question of gender, for it is the question of all our ordinary lives, men and women alike. The history of feminism begins precisely with the experience of inexpression, of which the theories of *care* give a concrete account in their ambition to valorize ignored, unexpressed dimensions of experience. This is the problem, beyond gender, that *care* confronts and which it allows to be presented without metaphysics. John Stuart Mill was concerned with the situation in which one does not have a voice for making oneself understood because one has lost contact with one's own experience:

> Thus the mind itself is bowed to the yoke: even in what people do for pleasure, conformity is the first thing thought of; they like in crowds; they exercise choice only among things commonly done: peculiarity of taste, eccentricity of conduct, are shunned equally with crimes: until by dint of not following their own nature, they have no nature to follow: their human capacities are withered and starved: they become incapable of any strong wishes or native pleasures, and are generally without either opinions or feelings of home growth, or properly their own. Now is this, or is it not, the desirable condition of human nature? (Mill, *On Liberty*, III)

This is a situation not specific to women, and which captures all situations of loss of experience and concepts together (and it can motivate a desire to come out of this situation, to repossess one's language, and to find a world that would be the adequate context for it).

To regain our contact with experience and to find a voice for its expression: this is the first aim, perfectionist and political, of ethics. It remains to articulate this subjective expression with the attention to the particular that is also at the heart of *care*, and thereby to define a *knowledge through care*. The moral knowledge, for example, that literature or cinema gives us through an education of our sensibility (sensitivity) cannot be translated into arguments but *is* nonetheless knowledge—hence the ambiguity of Nussbaum's title, *Love's Knowledge* (1990): not the knowledge of a general object, love, but the particular knowledge that a perception sharpened by love, or a sharpened perception of love, gives us. There is thus no contradiction between sensibility and knowledge, *care* and rationality. Ethics is an attention to others and to the manner in which they are, along with us, bound up in connections and practices. All ethics is thus an ethics of *care*, of the care for others.

Martha Nussbaum calls for a "perceptive equilibrium," parallel to Rawls's "reflective equilibrium," which could, like the "moral vision" she attributes to Henry James, produce an alternative to moral reasoning: "Novels construct the model of an ethical style of reasoning which is context-linked without being relativist, and which gives us concrete imperatives that can become universals" (Nussbaum, 2006, p. 8). Nussbaum nevertheless continues to refer to moral principles that are, to be sure, contextualized, but which are universalizable on the basis of concrete cases. She allows us to understand one of *care's* demands: through this "loving and attentive" reading, *caring*, we perceive moral situations differently, actively. This changes our perception of the responsibility of the moral agent and of agency. The attention to others that literature proposes to us does not give us new certainties, or the literary equivalent of theories; it puts us face to face with, in the grips of, an uncertainty, a perceptive *disequilibrium*. Diamond insists on the idea that human deliberation is "an *adventure* of the personality undertaken against terrific odds and among frightening mysteries" (Diamond, 1991, p. 313). By focusing on a narrow conception of ethics and of perception, one runs the risk of *bypassing the adventure*—missing a dimension of morality, and more specifically, the *face of moral thought*, "what moral life is *like*" (Diamond, 1991, p. 25). A dimension of morality is missed through lack of *care*.

Gilligan writes that a "restructuring of moral perception" should allow for "changing the meaning of moral language, and thus the definition of moral conflict and moral action" (1987, p. 43), but also for an undistorted vision of *care*, one in which *care* would not be the disappearance or diminution of the self. *Care*, understood as attention and perception, is to be differentiated from a sort of suffocation of the self by pure affectivity or devotion, as the oppositions *care/justice*, *care/rationality* could suggest. *Care*, by suggesting a new attention to the unexplored or neglected details of life, confronts us with our own inabilities and inattentions, but also, and above all, shows us how they are then translated into theory. In becoming political, what is at stake in ethics of *care* is epistemological: they seek to bring to light the connection between our lack of attention to neglected realities and the lack of theorization (or, more directly, the rejection of theorization) of these social realities, rendered invisible. Who has cleaned and straightened this room in which we are standing? Who is looking after my children right now?

From this perspective one may take up certain critiques brought against the ethics of care. Joan Tronto has suggested that the dyadic image of care (the amorous or maternal face-to-face) to which Gilligan remains attached is too narrow to include the ensemble of social activities that attentive care embraces. She considers that the philosophical valorization of *care* must base itself not so much in a particularist ethics but rather in an enlargement of the concept of action. This perhaps obliges one to give up on one part of the ethics of *care*, the idea of a specifically feminine ethics, and to join Tronto in moving towards a more gender-neutral anthropology. Gilligan's position was indissociable from a sexed anthropology: for her, the relationship to the self and to others as expressed in moral judgment took opposing directions for men and for women. According to Tronto, this position would inevitably lead to a sort of anthropological and political separatism of the genders. Against a sexed anthropology, she proposes an anthropology of needs, in order to found the social dignity of care. Not only do certain of our needs (and among the most important ones) call directly for care, but care defines the (political) space in which listening to needs becomes possible, as a veritable attention to others. In the end, the non-affectivist revival of *care* would call for an anthropology of vulnerability. *People are vulnerable*: it is this principle that definitively opens the space of needs and their consideration.

Reflection on *care* seems to oppose a feminine and a masculine conception of ethics, the first being defined by attention, care for the other, a sense of responsibility, and intimate connections; the second by justice and by autonomy. There is no need to emphasize the difficulty one would face in contrasting a feminine ethics and a masculine ethics, an ethics of care and an ethics of justice, and the risk one would run of reproducing the prejudices that the ethics of care (at first, as a feminist ethics) was precisely aimed at combating. For Tronto the idea that women have special moral qualities is quite misleading:

> As long as women's morality is categorized as a special kind of morality, then any argument made from 'women's morality' can be dismissed as irrelevant to the genuine concerns of 'real' or 'universal' morality. (…) One of my main targets in this book is a position that was current at the time, that there might be an alternative moral theory to adapt that grows out of women's experience, a position to signify that women occupy a moral 'high ground'. To me this argument is as one-sided as the argument that women are incapable of moral thought. (Tronto, 2009, p. 12-13)

One can, and as we shall see, Tronto does, integrate *care* into a general ethical, social, and political approach which would not be reserved for women, but which would be an aspiration for all, and would thus allow for an amelioration of the concept of justice.

One can, as others, like Nussbaum, Gilligan herself, and Diamond have suggested, redefine *care* and the just by redefining ethics on the basis of the sensible and of moral perception, something that has to do with a special expressivity of women.

Are these incompatible? Can the kind of new attention that *care* forces upon us be separated from the women's point of view? We should acknowledge the fact that women's voices have been deadened throughout history and that the ethics of care has given them an expression space. We see, however, that it is only in passing from ethics to politics that ethics of *care* can be given its critical power. By calling for a society in which *care-givers* would have their voice, their relevance, and in which the tasks of *care* would not be structurally invisible or inconspicuous, they bring to light the difficulty of thinking these social realities.

> Recognizing the importance of care would thus allow us to revalue the contributions made to human societies by the outcasts, by women, by the humble people who work everyday. Once we commit ourselves to remap the world so that their contributions count, then we are able to change the world. (Tronto, 2009, p. 15)

This connection between the ethics and politics of *care* is not the classical passage (already rightly criticized in Rawls) between a foundational ethics and its practical implementation. As Tronto puts it, the valorization of care passes through its *politicization* and voice. The ethical affirmation of the importance and dignity of *care* cannot go without a *political* reflection on the allocation of resources and the social distribution of tasks this allocation prescribes:

> As a type of activity, care requires a moral disposition and a type of moral conduct. We can express some of these qualities in the form of a universalist moral principle, such as: one should care for those around or in one's society. Nevertheless, in order for these qualities to become a part of moral conduct, people must engage in both private and public practices that teach them, and reinforce their senses of, these moral concerns. In order to be created and sustained, then, an ethic of care relies upon a political commitment to value care and to reshape institutions to reflect that changed value. (Tronto, 1993, p. 177-178)

Truly pursuing the ethics of *care* would imply both including practices linked to *care* in the agenda of democratic reflection and empowering those concerned—both care-givers and -receivers. This is what makes the ethics of care so difficult to grasp, even for feminists. The recognition of the theoretical pertinence of ethics of *care*, and the valorization of affections and affectivity—the importance of which we have seen in correcting a narrow vision of justice—necessarily pass through a practical revalorization of activities linked to care and a joint modification of intellectual and political agendas.

No ethics of care, then, without politics: Tronto is right, but we must perhaps also pursue the critical and radical—feminist—idea that was at the source of the ethics of *care* and of Gilligan's theses, which have been treated with such irony: the idea that dominant liberal (masculine, if one wishes) ethics are, in their political articulation, the product and expression of a social practice that devalorizes the attitude and work of *care*.

> The world of care, needless to say, has generally been ignored by social and political theorists. The world of care, needless to say, is often inhabited more thoroughly by women, people of lower class and caste status, working people, and other disregarded ethnic, religious, linguistic groups. They are the people most often excluded by politics. Even to bold thinkers who wanted to support the claims for women's greater public roles, such as Simone de Beauvoir, the vilification of the 'immanent' life continued. (Tronto, 2009, p. 15)

This perhaps allows one to begin to understand why theories of *care*, like many radical feminist theories, suffer from misrecognition: it is because a veritable ethics of *care* cannot exist without social transformation. The ethics of *care* gives concrete and ordinary questions—*who is taking care of whom, and how?*—the force and relevance necessary for critically examining our political and moral judgments.

II Ethics and What Matters

The aim of this chapter is to connect the ethics of care to the idea of the vulnerability of the human, as it is developed in the moral philosophy inspired by Wittgenstein. Stanley Cavell, Cora Diamond, and Veena Das work to link the very idea of the vulnerability of the human to a vulnerability of, if I may say, our life form(s). *Lebensformen* in Wittgenstein, as we have already explained, should be translated not by the phrase "forms of life," but "life forms." This idea of a life form is connected, for Cavell and Das, to Wittgenstein's anthropological sensitivity or sensibility, to his attention to everyday language forms, as being both obvious and strange, foreign.

To ask a question in the form of "In what circumstances would you say…?" is precisely Wittgenstein's most obvious (ordinary language) procedure directed to and *about us*, about us as philosophers when we are, as we inevitably are, variously tempted to force our ordinary words to do what they, as they stand, will not do, disappointed by finitude. It is *our* language that is, or that we perpetually render, foreign to us. (Cavell, preface to Das, 2007, p. iv). The uncanniness of the ordinary, for Cavell, is thus not resolved in the return to everyday life and words; the human is not a given, we do not know what it is:

> The blurring between what is human and what is not human shades into the blurring over what is life and what is not life. (Das, 2007, p. 16)

Attention to the everyday, to what Veena Das calls *the everyday life of the human*, is the first step in caring: care is attention, and the ethics of care calls our attention to phenomena commonly unseen, but that stand right before our eyes.

It also calls our attention to the moral capacities or competences of ordinary people. Here the definition of care by Joan Tronto and Berenice Fisher has to be taken very seriously:

> In the most general sense, care is a species of activity that includes everything that we do to maintain, continue, and repair our world so that we can live in it as well as possible. That world includes our bodies, our selves, our environment, all of which we seek to interweave in a complex, life sustaining web. (Fisher and Tronto, 1990, p. 40)

The perspective of *care* by calling our attention to our general situation of dependence, and to the danger of denying these connections, is thus indissociably political and ethical; it develops an analysis of social relations organized around dependence and vulnerability—blind spots of the ethics of justice. In response to the "original position" described by Rawls, the particular kind of realism lauded by the perspective of *care* would tend to set this "original condition"—to take Nel Noddings's terms (1984)—of vulnerability as the anchor point of moral and political thought. Thus the approaches of care target the theory of justice as it has developed and taken the dominant position in both political and moral fields of reflection over the course of the second half of the last century. This is not only because, as the controversies between the partisans of care and those of justice illustrate, these approaches call into question the universality of Rawls's conception of justice, but also because they transform the very nature of moral and social questioning and the very concept of justice. Care is a practice, not a moral feeling or disposition.

> Care is everywhere, and it is so pervasive a part of human life that it is never seen for what it is: activities by which we act to organize our world so that we can live in it as well as possible. When we get down to the ways that we actually live our lives, care activities are central and pervasive. How different the world looks when we begin to take these activities seriously. The world will look different if we place care, and its related values and concerns, closer to the center of human life. (Tronto, 2009, p. 14)

Care for the particular

A main difficulty of care, then, as a way of thinking about the world, is that

> This caring attitude requires us to reconcile the universal needs for care with the circumstances of what seems to be the best form of care in every individual case. It requires us to recognize that each and every one of us is not only the heroic decent caregiver, but we are also, in varying degrees through our lives but every day, also receivers of care. (Tronto, 2009, p. 15)

What is at stake in these discussions is the validity of general moral principles, hence, the relationship between the general and the particular. *Care* proposes bringing ethics back to the level of the "rough ground of the ordinary" (Wittgenstein, *Philosophical Investigations*), the level of everyday life. It is a practical response to specific needs, which are always those of singular others (whether close to us or not), of "the everyday life of the other;" it is work carried out just as much in the private sphere as in public; it a commitment not to treat anyone as insignificant, and it is a sensibility to the details that matter in lived situations. What is the pertinence, the importance of the particular, of individual sensibility? What can the singular claim? It is by giving back a (different) voice to the individual sensibility, to the intimate, that one ensures the conversation/conservation of a human world. This is something that is obvious in the contexts *Life and Words* accounts for, when violence destroys the everyday and the very sense of life as defining the human (Das, 2007, p. 89 Das 2020). Cavell refers to Das'

> recognition that in the gender-determined division of the work of mourning the results of violence, the role of women is to attend, in a torn world, to the details of everyday life that allow a household to function, collecting supplies, cooking, washing and straightening up, seeing to children, and so on, that allow life to knit itself back into some viable rhythm, pair by pair. Part of her task is to make us ponder how it is that such evidently small things (whose bravery within tumultuous circumstances is, however, not small) are a match for the consequences of unspeakable horror, for which other necessaries are not substitutes. (Cavell, preface to Das, 2007, p. xiii–xiv)

The subject of *care* is a sensible individual in as much as he or she is affected, is caught in a context of relations, in a *form of life* that is social and biological. He/she is attentive and considerate, and in so far as certain things, situations, moments or people count for him or her. The center of gravity of ethics is then shifted, from the "just" to the "important." Measuring the *importance* of care for human life means recognizing that dependence and vulnerability are not accidents that happen only to "others." See the title of the wonderful French movie: "Les gens normaux n'ont rien d'exceptionnel": similarly, "There is nothing exceptional about vulnerable people," Going against the grain of the ideal of autonomy animating most moral theories, *care* reminds us that we need others in order to satisfy our primordial needs. This unpleasant reminder may well be at the source of the misrecognition of *care*, reduced to a vacuous or condescending version of charity. We are unable to acknowledge that we need care.

The ideal of autonomy, even and maybe primarily for women, has defined a way of emancipation. The problem with autonomy is that it is made possible for actual individuals, today, through care. Care is not only for the sick and the elderly: for a woman or a man to be autonomous now means that one, or several, other people take care of her/him (cleaning, cooking, making calls, etc.). We do not like the idea; especially because it reminds us, also, that the emancipation of the Western woman (I am speaking here of the European situation) is due to the fact, not that men have really changed (as statistics about how much more domestic tasks they do at home illustrate), but that other women, from the South or the East, have taken over the tasks of care, which are still as invisible. Here, following Jean Tronto, I would like to suggest that the contempt for care ethics is actually grounded in a real contempt for the activities linked to *care*, and that only a reconsideration of the status of such activities would open a theoretical way to a philosophy of care.

Particularism and life forms

Reflection on *care* is part of the particularist turn in moral thought: against what Wittgenstein in the *Blue Book* called the "craving for generality"—the desire to pronounce general rules of thought and action—it is the attempt to valorize, within morality, attention to the particular(s), to the ordinary detail of human life, the neglected aspects. It is this descriptive aim that transforms morality: to learn to see what is important and unnoticed precisely because it is in front of our eyes. An ethics emerges of the particular perception of situations, of moments, of "what is going on," in the manner in which Erving Goffman defined the object of sociology in *Frame Analysis* (1974) and in which Hilary Putnam, also referring to Wittgenstein, spoke of an "ethics without ontology" (Putnam 2004). There are no univocal moral concepts that have only to be applied to reality, but rather, our moral concepts depend in their very application upon the narration or description we give of our existences, of what matters, and of what *counts* for us. This ability to perceive the importance of things, their place in our ordinary life, is not only affective, sensitivity: it is also the ability for adequate *expression* (or, equally, for a clumsy and awkward, failed expression). At the center of the ethics of *care* is our ability for (our disposition to) moral expression, which, as Cavell and Taylor have shown in various ways, is rooted in life forms, in the (Wittgensteinian) sense of a simultaneously natural and social aggregate of forms of expression and connection to others.

It is the form of life that determines the ethical structure of expression, and this expression, conversely, reworks it and gives it form. The relation to another, the type of interest and care we have for others, the importance we accord to them, take on their meaning only within the context of a possible unveiling (voluntary or involuntary) of oneself. Analyses in terms of *care* are inscribed within a critique of moral theory which claims the primacy of the description of moral practices in ethical reflection, calling into question the methodology, even the principle, of what G. E. M. Anscombe calls moral philosophy in her well-known article "Modern Moral Philosophy" (1958). Ethical theories are seen as abstract schemas supposed to guide the judgment of each and every one in such or such particular problem. They (like theories of justice) aim at conceiving and dealing with the particular on the basis of general rules or conceptions.

Practical ethics of care, on the other hand, start from concrete moral problems and see how we cope—not in order to abstract from these particular solutions (which would be to fall back into the craving for generality), but in order to perceive the value of (in) the particular. They call for a kind of moral ethnography—one which would make space for the expressions of agents themselves—rather than for an overarching theoretical approach. Conceiving morality on the model of justice and legality (a strong tendency in moral thought) leads to neglecting some of the most important and difficult aspects of moral life—our proximities, our motivations, our relations—in favor of concepts that are far removed from our ordinary questionings: such as obligation, rationality, choice.

Qualities such as *gentleness*, generosity, or kindness seem to escape available moral theories' capacities for description or appreciation. Michael Stocker noted that modern ethical theory has come to promote a petty and stunted moral life. Focusing on notions of rational action or moral choice (fertile as this may be) leaves out an important part of ordinary moral questioning and moral activities. It would be unfair to claim that contemporary moral reflection completely neglects qualities of this kind. But *care* aims to go further than ethics of virtues, for example, or ethics of human development/flourishing, would: it seeks to valorize care for others, not as against care for the self, but as the very basis for a real and realistic care for the self, acknowledged as vulnerable.

When Diamond affirms, in her introduction to *The Realistic Spirit* (1991, pp. 23-24), that moral philosophy has largely become "stupid and insensitive," she means insensitive to the human specificity of moral questioning, to this ordinary moral life bound up with others. For her, this is a matter of sensibility to what is said and to expression—a sensibility inherent to *care*—and would include those particular situations in which one cannot stand a certain attitude, or a certain vocabulary; when, faced with someone, one no longer wants to present arguments, and instead asks oneself, "Who is this person, in what world does he or she live, within what life can our discussion take place?" What matters is no longer the opposition between sensibility and understanding, but rather a conceptual sensibility, as thinkers such as J. McDowell have developed it (1994). The specifically sensible character of moral concepts and the perceptive character of conceptual activity is at work in *care*'s approach to the real.

Care and social justice

At the outset, and especially in the context of the *care*/justice discussion (which has become a thorny theme of American moral and political philosophy), the concern was the expression of a new approach, a new voice, one previously held at bay and reduced to silence. Carol Gilligan pointed out, in Kohlberg's model of moral development, the inability of the language of justice to take into account as morally pertinent the experiences and points of view of women: she hypothesized the "different voice" of a moral orientation that would identify and treat moral problems differently than the language of justice (Gilligan, 1982). This different orientation would have a coherence and validity of its own, which the language of care would allow one to grasp. Care analyses highlighting certain limits of ethics of justice are dedicated to this task of articulation and explication, of expression. These limits are traced out in terms of expression: ethics of care find a lack of awareness of a sensibility traditionally attributed to women, all the while signaling the conceptual and political difficulties of defining a feminine sensibility.

A properly political, and not only moral, stake of *care* is the introduction of a political dimension into family relations, into the private—into the intimate, where claims for equality seem inadequate, even within the couple. *Care* allows for taking into account the particularity of the relations of proximity that form within the family, and for re-examining the familial universe as an arena within which relations are shaped by tensions between sentiments of justice and love. By considering the social and affective conditions in which concrete modalities of care for others are deployed, the perspective of *care* opens out into a micro-politics of the arrangements between family members. As Margalit (2002) and Cavell (1981) maintain, the family, a pivotal institution in the distribution of cares and the division of the work of dependence, constitutes the first site for thought about care for others. The perspective of *care* then leads us to explore the ways in which we—in practice *and* in theory—treat the demarcation between the spheres of personal relations (familial relations, but also love, friendship, and affective relations in general) and the so-called impersonal spheres of public relations (this goes against Sennett and the idea of the "fall of public man").

The question is no longer one of choosing between *care* and justice, but of understanding how one can lose these two dispositions. Following Gilligan's suggestions in her recent writings:

> The potential error in justice reasoning lies in its latent egocentrism, the tendency to confuse one's perspective with an objective standpoint or truth, the temptation to define others in one's own terms by putting oneself in their place. The potential error in care reasoning lies in the tendency to forget that one has terms, creating a tendency to enter into another's perspective and to see oneself as 'selfless', by defining oneself in others' terms. (Gilligan, 1995, p. 43)

It is a matter, then, beyond the justice/care debate, of each individual's finding his or her voice, and of hearing both the voice of justice and that of *care*, avoiding these two errors and misunderstandings, these two distortions or deformations:

> the equation of human with male, unjust in its omission of women; and the equation of care with self-sacrifice, uncaring in its failure to represent the activity and the agency of care. (Gilligan, 1995, p. 43)

In order to legitimize the care approach it is thus necessary to return to the ordinary sense of justice, to the practice of care for others and for oneself. Care then appears as one of the existing paths towards a genuine ethics, one that is concrete and not normative. It is not a matter of making justice and sensibility compatible, in a sort of moralistic half-measure, of introducing a dose of care into the theory of justice, or on the contrary a measure of rationality to our affects. Numerous works in ethics have argued convincingly in favor of this compatibility. It is instead a matter, more radically, of seeing sensibility as a necessary condition of justice. Tronto notes that the care justice debate has in fact been "one sided": as if it were always the burden of the ethics of care to prove that it is compatible with justice. But shouldn't our standard theories of justice prove that they can take into account the needs of everyone? To account for "the everyday life of the other"?

The importance of importance

The ethics of care leads us to a completely different view of the aim of ethics, by drawing our attention to ordinary details of our lives, usually unseen. The philosophical craving for generality is "contempt for the particular case"; moral perception is care for the particular—coming to attention". (Cavell, 1981, p. 12)

This relationship between care and *what counts* was brought out by Cavell in regard to cinema and the films that *count* for us, and which are objects of our care:

> The moral I draw is this: the question what becomes of objects when they are filmed and screened—like the question what becomes of particular people, and specific locales and subjects and motifs when they are filmed by individual makers of film —has only one source of data for its answer, namely the appearance and significance of just these objects and people that are in fact to be found in the succession of films, or passages of films, that matter to us. (Cavell, 1984, p. 183)

The importance of cinema, of a certain moment in a film, is to be found in the way in which it brings out what is important, what counts. But

> if it is part of the grain of film to magnify the feeling and meaning of a moment, it is equally part of it to counter this tendency, and instead to acknowledge the fateful fact of a human life that the significance of its moments is ordinarily not given within the moments as they are lived, so that to determine the significant crossroads of a life may be the work of a lifetime. (Cavell, 1984, p. 11)

Care is defined on the basis of this specific attention to the *unseen* importance of things and moments, to the inherent concealment of importance. This fragility of the real and of experience, to speak in

Goffman's idiom (1987), is characteristic of ordinary experience, which is "structurally vulnerable" since its sense is never *given*. The redefinition of morality on the basis of importance and its connection to the structural vulnerability of experience could define the ethics of *care*.

The ethics of care as pragmatist feminism

My work on Wittgenstein, Austin, Cavell (Laugier, 2004, 2005, 2006, 2007a, 2007b, 2009, 2010, 2011) has meant opening new ethical perspectives on the theme of the *ordinary*: to show the relevance of ordinary language philosophy for ethical and political issues, developing an ordinary conception of politics in thinking on civil disobedience and democracy (Ogien & Laugier 2010, 2014), and an ordinary conception of ethics in thinking of care and gender. It means including women (all women) in the public conversation. The question of the ordinary is anchored in ordinary language philosophy, the "rough ground" of the uses and practices of language; it leads to further investigating the denial or undervaluation of the ordinary. The ordinary is variously undervalued, or neglected (not seen, not taken into account) in theoretical thought, just as the mass of ordinary people is not taken into account in political conversation (that is the origin of civil disobedience and mobilizations), and women do not matter in a just proportion to their number, in all democracies. Such negligence (*carelessness*) has to do with contempt for ordinary forms of life inasmuch as they are domestic, female, even among liberals or feminists; and is connected to or stems from a gendered hierarchy of the objects of intellectual research, which parallels and reinforces social hierarchies and binaries. Inclusion of women in the political sphere (hence in the public) is less than obvious and not assured for most of (non-feminist) political philosophy.

In face of this situation, the idea of an ethics formulated *in a different voice* is: 1) an ordinary conception of ethics; 2) an expressivist conception of ethics; 3) a pragmatic conception of ethics. This ethics is not founded on universal principles but starts from experiences of everyday life and the moral problems of humans, of women in their ordinary lives. The notion of care is best expressed not in the form of a theory, but an activity: care as action (taking care, caring for) and as attention, concern (caring about). Care is at once a practical response to specific needs, which are always those of individual, singular others (whether close or not)—an activity necessary to maintaining persons and connections, work carried out both in the private sphere and in the public sphere, and sensitivity to what matters. Care is a concrete matter, embedded in the ordinary details of human life, ensuring the maintenance (in several senses, including the sense of conversation and conservation) and continuity of the human world. This ethics is based on an analysis of the historical conditions that have favored a division of moral labor such that activities of care have been socially and morally devalorized. The assignment of women to the domestic sphere has reinforced the exclusion of these activities and preoccupations from the moral domain and the public, reducing them to the rank of private sentiments devoid of moral and political import, and keeping the great majority of women secluded from the public (even defined in the terms we have here).

This is the definition of ethics (a paradigm shift) that is deeply connected to attention to, care for, repossession of, ordinary language, and that transforms the very notion of ethics, enhancing the question of human vulnerability, and connecting it to the vulnerability of language use; but it also opens ethics to a democratic challenge.

The idea of an ethics formulated in a "different voice" (Carol Gilligan's method)—a woman's voice—follows on these explorations of OLP, using Carol Gilligan's approach and connecting it to OLP. Care is a practical response to specific needs and a sensitivity to the ordinary details and textures of human life that *matter*. Hence, care is a concrete matter that ensures maintenance (for example, as conversation and conservation) and continuity of the human world and form of life. A form of life, from the point of view of ethics, can be grasped only by attention to textures or moral patterns, perceived as "morally expressive" in/on the background provided by a form of life. Contextualism means elements of the moral vocabulary have no sense except in the context of a form of life. Words come to life against the background that "gives our words their sense." When Wittgenstein says: "Only in the practice of a language can a word have meaning," he means that sense is determined not only by use or "context" (as many analyses of language have recognized) but also that sense is embedded in and only perceptible against the background of the practice of language.

Care can be thus conceived as the *protection of form of life*. This appears clearly in contexts in which violence destroys the everyday, and the sense of life; disaster.

The ethics of care has contributed to modifying a dominant conception of ethics, and changed profoundly the way we look at ethics, or what ethics should look like. Care is a fundamental aspect of human life, a set of various practices and feelings, and an ethics. Care consists of "everything we do to continue, repair, and maintain ourselves so that we can live in the world as well as possible" (Tronto & Fisher, 1990, p. 41). The subject of care is a sensible, passive individual inasmuch as he or she is affected, is caught in a context of relations, in a form of life that is indissolubly social and biological, relations and hierarchies that pervade our lives—what Foucault defines in terms of a *biopolitics*.

Measuring the *importance* of care for human life means recognizing the possibility of a subjectivity defined not by agency or self-assertion or autonomy, but by dependence and vulnerability. Going against the grain of the ideal of autonomy animating most moral and political theories, including many feminist theories, the ethics of care reminds us that we need others in order to satisfy our primordial needs even (and even more) when we display obvious autonomy. (Humanist African philosophy refers to core concept of *ubuntu*, derived from the Zulu phrase "*Umuntu ngumuntu ngabantu*", which means that a person is a human because of others.) This unpleasant reminder may well be at the source of the misrecognition of care, often reduced to a vacuous or condescending version of charity. We are unable to acknowledge that we need care, constantly, and not only as infants and ill or elderly. Precariousness and vulnerability are features of the human life form. Ethics is not about living a good or right life, making the right choices, but just about living a life, and this transforms ethics towards the descriptive.

OLP, and the discovery of speech acts in particular, has been connected to this problematic of failure, of transgression, and of the vulnerability of the human person. Excuses —*what we say* when it appears that we have acted badly (clumsily, inadequately, etc.)—are the site of vulnerability of language. Action, Austin notes, is something specifically human: vulnerability as defined by the "linguistic constellation of excuses. Austin presents the complexity of human actions and of their possible classifications in terms of excuses. The diversity of excuses shows the diversity and variety of actions, and for any given excuse there is a limit to the acts for which it will be accepted: what Austin calls norms of the unacceptable. This is part of a description of human form of life as vulnerable. Austin shows the vulnerability of ordinary human action, defined, just as the performative utterance, as what can go wrong, and the vulnerability of human social life: action is structured by language, defined and regulated by failure, by going wrong. Austin, like Goffman, aims to set out the conditions of felicity of language as an ordinary practice, to make clear the vulnerability of our usages, and to specify certain adequate tools of compensation for our misses. Austin in *Sense and Sensibilia*, mentioning "mis-readings, mishearings, Freudian slips etc." stating there is no clear dichotomy between "*things going right and things going wrong: things may go wrong, as we really all know quite well, in lots of different ways*" (Austin 1964, p. 13; cf. conclusion of "Pretending", Austin's general project of describing the failures of human agency).

The ordinary form of life is vulnerable—to others, to ourselves, and to our mistakes. Things can permanently *go wrong*. Goffman defines the human character of action in the same way. We find the coupling of failure and excuse, of offense and compensation, in Goffman's analyses, in his examples of failures and inappropriate behavior. Attention to excuses and to the compensation due to others is an essential connection between Austin and Goffman, especially in Goffman's later major work, *Frame Analysis: An Essay on the Organization of Experience* (1974). The point is to *see* the human form of life as vulnerable, defined by a constellation of possibilities of failure, of ways we have to make amends, of strategies we can use to forgive or forget.... These phenomena make us feel the fragility of ordinary life form and make us feel our vulnerability in the presence of others. Excuses, in their permanent recognition of human vulnerability, place the ordinary in the realm of the tragic (Cavell 1994), disaster (Lovell et al., 2013), what is *threatened*.

> When an incident occurs and spontaneous involvement is threatened, then reality is threatened.... The minute social system, that is brought into being with each encounter, will be disorganized, and the participants will feel unruled, unreal, and anomic. (Goffman, 2005, p. 135)

Comparably, the activity of reparation of offense, for Goffman, is undertaken in the context of this radical vulnerability, which is equally manifest in small, everyday offenses (the word of excuse that doesn't come, the absence of attention) as in tragedy. Goffman's *misframing* connects to Austin's misperception. His question "What is it that's going on here?" is an echo of Austin's "What should we say when...?" Reality itself is vulnerable to our mistakes, re-readings and interpretations, to our misperceptions and carelessness, and it is this very vulnerability that defines the ordinary form of life.

This is something obvious in the contexts Das's *Life and Words* accounts for, when violence destroys the everyday and the sense of life as defining the human. In Swapan's story, as told by Das in *Affliction* (2015), care is care for the preservation of form of life, life—biological and social—being threatened by madness. The threat to normality (normal family life) becomes a threat to reality itself. We can use here what Goffman says in "The Insanity of Place" (*Psychiatry*, 32, p. 257) about the unreality of life as it is remembered (as a dream) after the crisis created by the occurrence of madness in a family. But this unreality appears in ordinary incidents.

We can connect the ethics of care to the idea of the vulnerability of human life form. The uncanniness of the ordinary, for Cavell, is then not resolved in the return to everyday life and words; the human, or life, is not a given—it is defined by the permanent threat of denial of the human, of dehumanization/devitalization. Attention to what Das calls *the everyday life of the human* is the first step in caring: care is attention, and the ethics of care call our attention to phenomena commonly unseen, but who stand right before our eyes ("voir le visible," Foucault, 1978) and to human capacities for expression and claim. The ethics of care merges with sensitivity to words by drawing our attention to the place of ordinary words in the weave and details of our life forms.

Care is just what makes ordinary form of life possible. Tronto and Fisher suggest that care is a generic activity meaning all what we do in order to perpetuate and repair our "world," so that we can live in it as well as it possible. "This 'world' includes our bodies, our environment, and ourselves" (1990, p. 40). Ethics, then, is not about how to live better or more virtuous or rational lives, but how, simply, for anyone to live an ordinary life in the world.

> *The world is our home.* Human life, we must assume in the first place, is somewhat more important than anything else in human life, except, possibly, what happens to it. It deserves attention, and a seriousness of attention, commensurate with its importance.... A civilization which for any reason puts a human life at a disadvantage; or a civilization which can exist only by putting human life at a disadvantage, is worthy neither of the name nor of continuance. (Agee, 2013, p. 34)

Standard ethics, and political analysis, when they deal with the social contract, do not inquire into how such a society is made sustainable, carefully expelling from ethics the world of care, and more generally speaking all those actions that make ordinary social and moral relations possible and alive. Ignoring the care issue in ethics and politics amounts to ignoring the origin of what enables a moral society to exist and perpetuate.

III Care and Ordinary Language Philosophy

This chapter is meant to strengthen the connection I have wanted to establish since the publication of my first writings on the concept of care (Paperman & Laugier, 2005) (Laugier, 2014), between the ethics of care and ordinary language philosophy, as represented by Wittgenstein, Austin, Cavell, and thus to find some resources in OLP, often considered disconnected from gender issues (except through speech acts theory), for a reformulation of what is at stake, or important, for me, in feminism. This has to be put in context. My (and my students') work on Wittgenstein, Austin, and Cavell has meant to open new perspectives in France on the neglected question, or the theme, of the *ordinary*: early on I wanted to show the relevance of ordinary language philosophy for ethical and political issues (for example, developing an ordinary conception of politics in thinking on civil disobedience and radical democracy, Laugier 2004, 2010, 2014). My aim is to open a systematic exploration of the (theoretical and practical) question of the *ordinary* on the basis of ordinary language philosophy, the "rough ground" of the uses and practices of language—by further investigating the denial or undervaluation of the ordinary in contemporary thought, and by examining concretely the forms in which this undervaluation appears in various bodies of work, mostly philosophical

In order to do this, I am using ordinary language philosophy (OLP) as a basis for a re-definition of ethics as attention to ordinary life and care for moral expression.

My guiding idea is that while the *ordinary*, often an object of interest and even fascination within contemporary thought, is variously denied, undervalued, or neglected (not seen, not taken into account) in theoretical thought as well as in the collection of data, a reconsideration of the ordinary through OLP has a critical and ethical impact, and relevance for feminism. The negligence (*carelessness*) towards the ordinary has to do with contempt for ordinary life inasmuch as it is domestic, female, and stems from gender categories, or from a hierarchy of the objects of intellectual research, which is again a gendered one.

1. The importance of OLP: linguistic phenomenology

The starting point for the project of my book *Du réel à l'ordinaire Quelle philosophie du langage aujourd'hui ?* (1999) and now translated *From the Real to the Ordinary* (2013c) was the idea of a philosophy of language anchored not (or not only) in the standard model of analytic philosophy, nor in continental philosophy but rather in a philosophy attentive to the uses of language, to language as it is used, in use, in circulation. I have developed this point at length in my works on Wittgenstein and Austin, and in the work of the students I have trained in this area. My goal from here forward was to join these theories of the ordinary to practices of the ordinary, and to discover and elucidate ordinary theories in the immanence of practices—not by proposing "theories of practice," but rather "ordinary theories": the thought that emerges within these practices, or the intelligence these practices contribute to their own realization.

Thus, with new conceptual tools (not only Cavell, my resource for years, but also Dewey's pragmatism, and care ethics) I hope to pursue a project to highlight the power—not only formational or emotional, but also theoretical and cognitive—of "ordinary" materials: everyday conversations, ordinary expressiveness, or "popular culture." My research on OLP was focused on ordinary realism and aimed to show language as a fine, precision tool for describing reality (by proposing the ideas of adjustment and the perception of differences and resemblances in order to account for realist aspirations), but this focus was inseparable from recognition of the fact that language is part of the world, and that we use it in everyday life, in our conversations. The meaning of ordinary language philosophy does indeed lie in this recognition that language is used, spoken by a human voice. This sense of language is what the second Wittgenstein means by "form of life": the question is no longer whether language is an image of reality, but to "come back to earth" and to see the practices in which language is *caught* and which collect around our words. So this makes OLP an alternative political and ethical approach.

OLP is a minority and truly alternative current in the mainstream philosophy of language and even in the active and recognized field of pragmatics. The importance of this philosophical current can indeed be seen in political terms, through an analysis and re-evaluation of its arguments, and through a re-reading of the "official" history of analytic philosophy. The analytic philosophy that emerged from the "linguistic turn." now a dominant strand linked to the cognitive sciences and the so-called "philosophy of mind," is certainly fertile and has allowed for some innovative scientific interactions. Nevertheless, the standard program of analytical philosophy has systematically neglected important and vibrant contemporary currents that have emphasized and developed a philosophy of language irreducible to cognitivist models, and attentive to everyday usages of language.

OLP takes ordinary uses of language as the starting point for philosophical analysis, considering that this is a condition for avoiding the "scholastic illusion" denounced by Austin in the 1950s and later by Bourdieu, which consists in taking "the things of logic for the logic of things" (Bourdieu 1990) and often leads to thought becoming sterilized in vain scholasticism that loses all connection to the problems posed in ordinary life or in concrete research. Thus, it is from the outset oriented towards the social matters. Its primary methodological ambition is a conceptual analysis that makes it possible to recognize the importance of context in the practice of language, thought, and perception—that is, in our different ways of engaging in the real—while at the same time defending a non-metaphysical form of realism, anchored in agents' practices: their words, expressions, and thoughts.

It is the inspiration for today's current of "contextualism" in philosophy of language and philosophy of knowledge (Recanati 2004; Travis 1989, 2001). In my opinion, this development of contextualism or even "relativism" has ignored some important aspects of OLP: its ambition to describe, as precisely as possible, the cognitive, perceptual, linguistic, social, and moral dimensions of our usages and an analysis of all forms of expression—not only descriptive and performative, but also emotional or passionate. The domain of the perlocutionary is in particular a sort of "black continent," which, with the exceptions of Stanley Cavell, Nancy Bauer, Alice Crary and Richard Moran, has not been explored in philosophical literature.

With the Austinian notion of linguistic phenomenology, OLP orients its reflection on language towards a type of adequacy that is no longer correspondence (either in metaphysical terms or in terms of a philosophy of mind), but rather the fineness of adjustment as a function of the perception of differences. It must be understood that OLP does not encourage defining the meaning of a term as the set of situations in which this term is appropriate or as a pack of established uses (an erroneous understanding of Wittgenstein and his definition of meaning as use), but rather to examine how meaning is improvised, created by its integration into practice and self-expressivity. This is the as yet unexplored path I want to pursue: an experience of words and language as part of the real and as affecting us, allowing us to affect others, and as constantly transforming meaning. Linguistic phenomenology means to pay attention to words, but always as being able to establish new meanings. In return, we get a "sharpened awareness" (Austin, 1962a) of words and what they are about (thus, reality). The agreement at the heart of linguistic phenomenology is not the correspondence between words and things (formal, or term to term), but rather the agreement between ourselves, what we mean (Cavell, 1969), and reality. It completes the political agreement in language, which is not a consensus. My agreement or my belonging to *this or that* form of life, political or moral, is not given. The form of this acceptance, the limits and scales of our agreement, are not knowable *a priori*, "no more than one can *a priori* know the scope or scale of a word" (Cavell, 1989), and this is essential to the social relevance of OLP (see Norris, 2006).

> There is a pervasive and systematic background of agreements among us, which we had not realized, or had not known we realize. Wittgenstein sometimes calls them conventions, sometimes rules.... The agreement we act upon he calls 'agreement in judgments' (§242), and he speaks of our ability to use language as depending upon agreement in 'forms of life' (§241). But forms of life, he says, are exactly what have to be 'accepted'; they are 'given'. (Cavell, 1979, p. 30)

That we agree in language means that language—our form of life—produces our understanding of one another just as much as language is a product of agreement, that it is *natural* to us in this sense. OLP appears not as a deviation from the philosophy of language, but its pure form, the maintenance of an initial claim:

> When we examine what we should say when, what words we should use in what situations, we are looking again not *merely* at words (or 'meanings' whatever they may be) but also at the realities we use the words to talk about: we are using a sharpened awareness of words to sharpen our perception of, though not as the final arbiter of, the phenomena. (Austin, 1962b, p. 182)

Words, says Austin, are "middle-sized dry goods," typical of our ordinary objects, and we are in touch with them, so this tangible relation we have to our words is something that connects OLP and attention to literature and to the general question of sensibility to words (see Moi, 2005; Cavell, 1969). This is how OLP led me to two main directions of thought involving gender and feminism, attention to women's voices: women's ordinary expressiveness, and the ethics of care that was at the outset a claim for the validity of women's voice, a different voice (Gilligan, 1982).

It is one of Austin's intuitions through to the end: we must not concern ourselves only with the analysis of what we say, but with the *we* and with the *should* and the *say*. *Must We Mean What We Say?* (Cavell, 1969) was the first work to ask the question of the *relevance* of our statements as relevance *in relation to ourselves*, in various domains and by turning to unexpected resources (literature, art criticism). This new (heterodox) notion of relevance is what needs to be explored from now on, as an alternative to its mentalist version. The content (objective, semantic, or empirical) of propositions is no longer the question, nor is the much-discussed "nonsense," but rather the fortunes and misfortunes of ordinary expression. "The statements fit the facts always more or less loosely, in different ways on different occasions for different intents and purposes" (Austin, 1962b, p. 130)—what matters here then, is the search for (or loss of) the right tone or right word, conceptually, morally, socially, and sensibly. It is a matter of finding the fine sensibility to things and the adjustment of words within ordinary uses and connections. The question is: how can I know if I adequately project the words I have learned into new contexts? (Cavell, 1979; Travis 1989; Laugier 1999-2013). There is an "unhappy" dimension, a dimension of failure in Ordinary language philosophy, which is obsessed with cases where our words fail, are inadequate, inexpressive, inarticulate (see Austin, 1962; Goffman, 1987).

It then remains to navigate between the Austinian critique of expression (as stemming from psychology) and caricatural forms of emotivism, which separate the content of our words from the emotion "associated" with them. It is, in the end, a matter of an indissolubly aesthetic and moral problem: to articulate in women's voice, the rightness of tone, adequacy of expression to self-knowledge (or self-confidence). This articulation of the linguistic and the moral is what could be explored through the question of women's expressiveness and through a return to the analysis of the perlocutionary that would escape both the conformism of pragmatics and other uses of Austin in terms of non-linguistic "performance" (1962a).

2. Care and the different voice

Introducing the ethics of care in France has been an interesting experience. I meant it as developing a heterodox ethics, inspired by approaches in moral sociology, and moral perfectionism (Laugier, 2010), but above all, as a matter of continuing OLP by other means— by re-centering moral philosophy on ordinary language and expressiveness. From this comes the idea of an ethics formulated *in a different voice* and expressed in a feminine voice, as can be examined, for example, in literary and cinematographic bodies of work. In this ordinary conception of ethics, morality is not founded on universal principles but rather starts from experiences of everyday life and the moral problems of real people in their ordinary lives. The notion of care is best expressed not in the form of a theory, but of an activity: for example, care as action (taking care, caring for) and as attention, concern (care about). Care is at once a practical response to specific needs, which are always those of individual, singular others (whether close or not)—an activity necessary to maintain persons and connections, work carried out both in the private sphere and in the public sphere, and sensitivity to the "details" that matter. This is the definition of ethics (which may be called a paradigm shift) that is deeply connected to attention to, and repossession of, ordinary language, and that transforms the very notion of ethics, enhancing the question of human vulnerability but also the philosophical resistance to such a transformation.

The (polemical) importance of the ethics of care is that, just as OLP does, it subverts well-established intellectual and social hierarchies and attracts attention to a number of phenomena that are overlooked because they are connected to the female. It is a matter of showing that the (moral) sentiments of women are not an inferior level of morality, but a moral resource that has been ignored, and which would make it possible to profoundly renew moral and social thought. This is on condition of seeing care not only as a sensibility or a sub-theory but also as an ordinary practice, an ethics defined not by abstract principles but by the concrete work done for the most part by women, and neglected because of it. In fact, taking into consideration the social, moral, and political importance of care makes it necessary to refer to "women," one of the categories to which the work of care has principally been assigned, which has led to it being criticized as "differentialist." We can hope to go beyond this prejudice and to return to the question of universalism, the critique by care ethics of the incapacity of the language of justice to take into account women's ordinary experiences and points of view as morally relevant and different (Zerilli, 2009). The hypothesis of a "different voice" is indeed that of a moral orientation that identifies and treats moral problems differently than the language of justice and liberal moral philosophy do. The ethics of care has for me contributed to this transformation of ethics and voice. By proposing to valorize moral values like caring, attention to others, solicitude, the ethics of care has contributed to modifying a dominant conception of ethics, and changed fundamentally the way we look at ethics, or how ethics should look. It has introduced ethical stakes into politics, weakening through its critique of theories of justice the seemingly obvious link between an ethics of justice and political liberalism.

Care corresponds to a quite ordinary reality: the fact that people look after one another, take care of one another, and thus are attentive to the functioning of the world, which depends on this kind of care. Ethics of care affirms the importance of care and attention given to others, in particular to those whose lives and wellbeing depend on particularized, continual, and daily attention: ordinary vulnerable others. Ethics of care draws our attention to the ordinary, to what we are unable to see, but is right before our eyes. An ethics that gives voice and attention to humans that are undervalued precisely because they accomplish unnoticed, invisible tasks, and take care of the basic needs of others.

This ethics is based on an analysis of the historical conditions that have favored a division of moral labor such that activities of care have been socially and morally devalorized. The assignment of women to the domestic sphere has reinforced the exclusion of these activities and preoccupations from the moral domain and the public sphere, reducing them to the rank of private sentiments devoid of moral and political import. The perspectives of care carry with them a fundamental claim concerning the importance of care for human life, for the relations that organize it, and the social and moral position of caregivers. To recognize this means recognizing that dependence and vulnerability are traits of a condition common to all, not of a special category—the "vulnerable." This sort of "ordinary" realism (in the sense of "realistic" proposed by Diamond, 1991) is absent from the majority of social and moral theories, which have a tendency to reduce the activities and preoccupations of care to a concern for victims and for the weak on the part of selfless mothers. Hence the importance of acknowledging the first import of the ethics of care: *the human is vulnerable*. So vulnerability defines ordinariness and the development of the concept of vulnerability provides new resources for a reevaluation of the ordinary.

OLP helps us connect the ethics of care to the idea of the vulnerability of the human, as it is developed in the ethics inspired by Wittgenstein. Cavell, Diamond, and Veena Das work to connect the very idea of the vulnerability of the human to a vulnerability of, if I may say, our life form(s). *Lebensformen* in Wittgenstein, Cavell stresses, should be translated not by the phrase "forms of life," but life forms (Cavell, 1979). This idea of a life form is connected, for Cavell and Das, to Wittgenstein's anthropological sensitivity or sensibility, to his attention to everyday language forms, as being both obvious and strange, foreign. Care is definitely attention, and the ethics of care calls our attention to phenomena commonly unseen, but that stand right before our eyes.

To define ethics by this immanent caring also calls our attention to the moral capacities or competences of ordinary people. Attention to the everyday, to what Veena Das calls *the everyday life of the human*, the *ordinary other*, is the first definition of caring.

Reflection on care can be construed as a consequence, or even as a part of the turn in moral thought illustrated by the work of Diamond (1991) and Crary (2007): against what Wittgenstein in the *Blue Book* called the "craving for generality"—the desire to pronounce general rules of thought and action. It is the attempt to valorize, within morality, attention to the particular(s), to the ordinary detail of human life, the neglected aspects. It is this descriptive aim that transforms morality: to learn to see what is important and unnoticed precisely because it is in front of our eyes.

There are no univocal moral concepts that have only to be applied to reality, but rather, our moral concepts depend in their very application upon the narration or description we give of our existences, of what matters, and of what *counts* for us. This ability to perceive the importance of things, their place in our ordinary life, is not only affective, sensitivity: it is also the ability for adequate *expression* (or, equally, for a clumsy and awkward, failed expression). It is the form of life that determines the ethical structure of expression, and this expression, conversely, reworks it and gives it form. The relation to the other, the type of interest and care we have for others, the importance we accord to them, take on their meaning only within the context of a possible unveiling (voluntary or involuntary) of oneself.

This idea of *Lebensform* is associated in Cavell (1979) and Das (2007) with attention to the ordinary form of life: to what Cavell calls "the uncanniness of the ordinary" and Das "the everyday life of the human." Care is, first, attention to ordinary human life in its vulnerability. The ethics of care calls our attention to what is just in front of our eyes but which we do not see because of a lack of attention or because it is too close. Care is defined on the basis of the specific attention to the *invisible* importance of things and moments: what Cavell calls "the essential dissimulation of importance" (Cavell, 2003, p. 11), which is part of what cinema also teaches us about our ordinary life. Cavell, in his work on film and his autobiography, *Little Did I Know*, notes that the importance of film lies in its power to make what matters emerge: "to magnify the feeling and meaning of a moment" (1984, p. 11). Film cultivates in us a specific ability to see the invisible importance of things and moments, and emphasizes the covering over of importance in ordinary life. For importance is essentially what can be *missed*, what remains unseen until later, or possibly, forever. The pedagogy of film is that while it amplifies the significance of moments, it also reveals the "inherent concealment of significance." Acknowledging the importance of the ordinary is a crucial part of Cavell's contribution to feminism. Experience reveals itself as defined by our quasi-cinephiliac capacity for seeing detail, reading expressions. The structure of expression articulates the concealment *and* the revelation of importance, and such is the texture of life.

This is the difficulty that Cavell describes when he speaks of the temptation of inexpressiveness and of isolation, and shows the essential vulnerability and passiveness of human experience (another name for skepticism, and expressed in the genre of the "melodrama of the unknown woman"). Failure to pay attention to importance, it turns out, is as much a moral failure as it is a cognitive one. Yet we discover importance not only through accurate and refined perception, but through our suffering and misperception, in other words, through our failures to perceive. Because "missing the evanescence of the subject" (Cavell, 1984, p. 14) is constitutive of our ordinary lives—as well as being the ordinary truth of skepticism. Acknowledging this consequence of skepticism, our inevitable failure to "appreciate the situation" and perceiving importance, is a step toward genuine attention to ordinary life.

Redefining morality on the basis of *importance* and on the link between morality and the structural vulnerability of the human experience may thus help in rethinking the theoretical stakes of the ethics of care. The notion of care is inseparable from a cluster of terms, a particular language game: attention, concern, importance, meaning, mattering (Cavell 1981; Laugier 2011). This attention results from the development of a perceptive ability to see how a detail or an expressive gesture stands out against a background. The notion of care refers to an ordinary reality, one we do not see, precisely because it is defined by invisibility (Wittgenstein's method again). The notion of care points to a specific blindness in contemporary moral and political thought: blindness to the conditions of its own development within the human form of life.

Ethics of care, by opening ethics to ordinary voices in their diversity, is a criticism of a dominant (male) understanding of ethics, by placing vulnerability at the heart of morality. It joins up with Wittgensteinian ethics (Diamond 1991, 2011; Crary 2007), and with ecofeminism and disability studies, which connect the vulnerability of the human with a vulnerability of the human form of life.

Care is a subversion of intellectual and ethical hierarchies. The perspective of care then leads us to explore the ways in which we, in practice *and* in theory, treat the demarcation between the spheres of personal relations (familial relations, but also love, friendship) and the so-called impersonal spheres of public relations, with of course a hierarchy involved: so the political stakes in the ethics of care is again the ethical enablement of populations and categories that are assumed as morally inferior.

> The traditional association of caring with women rested on a social order that excluded women from many parts (or all) of the public sphere. Women (and for that matter slaves, servants, and often working-class people) as well as care activities were relegated outside of public life. One of the great accomplishments of the second wave of feminism was to break the caste barriers that excluded women from the public sphere. (Tronto, 2005, p. 130)

OLP could help us to go beyond the notion of care and, in the line of thought represented by Das (2007), Nussbaum (2011), and Sen (2009), to engage in reconceiving ethics, not on the basis of grand principles, but rather of the fundamental needs of humans and women. More generally, this ethical reflection is linked to the definition, developed by Diamond, Nussbaum, Moi, of ethical competence in terms of a refined and active perception, which certainly has not been pursued in all its feminist consequences and especially the analysis it provides of differences and inequalities among women created by care networks and relationships. The ethics of care, by suggesting a new attention to unexplored details or neglected elements of life, confronts us with our own inabilities and inattentiveness, but also with how these things are translated into theory. The stakes of ethics of care end up epistemological by becoming political: ethics of care seeks to highlight the connection between our lack of attention to neglected realities and the lack (or more directly, the rejection) of theorization of these social realities rendered "invisible," and in this way to understand why ethical, and often philosophical, thought is blind to certain ordinary realities, in particular those connected with the domain of the private, the domestic, and the feminine. Thus we find the continuation of the OLP project formulated by Wittgenstein: "What we are supplying are really remarks on the natural history of human beings ... observations which no one has doubted, but which have escaped remark only because they are always before our eyes" (*Philosophical Investigations*, §415). On the ethical level as well, the ordinary is defined within this difficulty in accessing what is just before our eyes, which we must learn to see.

Gilligan has claimed the generality of her approach: justice and care are two different tonalities, or rival voices, existing inside each of us, the care voice being less inhibited in girls than in boys. The notion of care, in as much as it covers very practical activities and a form of sensitivity, a sustained attention to others and a sense of responsibility and dependence, subverts theories of impartial justice. The ethics of care does not aim at instilling pity, compassion, solicitude and benevolence as subsidiary values that would lessen the harshness of a cold conception of social relations, an impartial conception of justice based on the primacy of rights attributed to autonomous, separated, rational individuals. Such a description would better suit what is called solicitude, that is to say, care from the perspective of justice or as it appears in that political discourse whose the target it has been since its appearance.

Attention to ordinary expression (for example, within popular film or television series) leads to re-considering the question of a properly feminine expression, one which has been stifled or neglected and which finds its place in films and especially in series centered on strong female main characters, whom viewers come to know by spending time observing them (*Buffy the Vampire Slayer*, *Desperate Housewives*, *Damages*, *Weeds*, *Orange is the New Black*, *Homeland*, *The Handmaid's Tale*...).

Another interesting aspect is the possibility of displacing gendered hierarchies of aesthetic interests by bringing out not only the moral and intellectual value of ordinary practices, but also of the ordinary theories immanent in these practices.

Once again, ordinary language is not to be envisioned as having only a descriptive, or even agentive, function, but as a perceptual instrument that allows for fineness and adjustment in perceptions and actions. Such an imbrication of cognition, perception, and expression is illustrated in moral situations, that is to say, in the perception of ordinary situations and moral expressions. Moral sensitivity is thus an essential element of all communication, and the reader-viewer's acquisition of this competence can be the object of moral analyses (see Nussbaum 1990; Diamond, 1997; Crary, 2007; Laugier, 2006). This makes it possible to go beyond classical moral conceptions, which are based on choice, in a new way, and to imagine different moral approaches: people's ways of being, natural expressions and reactions, the moving texture of personalities, the constitution of characters over the long term, the expression of a vision of the world through speech and personal style.

I want to insist again on Cavell's contribution to the question of what it is to be a woman, and to gender studies, with his elaboration of the concepts of expression and voice; concepts which are in my reading here most crucial to Cavell's philosophy of language and OLP.

Many commentators have noted Cavell's relevance, especially of his classic work on film—Hollywood remarriage comedy and melodrama—for gender issues and what he calls "the history of women." This relevance is grounded on a conception of voice, expression, and in general on a conception of language connected not only, as has been mentioned earlier, to ordinary use and forms of life, but also to the essential vulnerability of meaning and expression—and to the constant threat of inexpressiveness. This is obvious when one considers the place Cavell gives to Hollywood films in the creation of a new woman, and the emergence of a generation of women: the films studied in *Pursuits of Happiness* (1981) were written and shot and presented to the public at a historical moment (the 30s-40s) when, after the emergence of great figures in feminism, and notable gains since 1848, culminating in winning the vote for women in 1920, it became obvious that women needed—still need—"more than rights": actual equality, equality in voice. Cavell's contribution is his study of film at the beginning of the talking movies, to show that what women want is not "only" citizenship equality, but equality of voice, which comes through a fuller expression: conversational equality (which is claimed, but not always won, in the conversations and arguments in the movies) and speech equality in general. The women/actresses in the films (for example, Katharine Hepburn, Irene Dunne, Barbara Stanwyck) represent an extraordinary generation of women, capable of giving new expression to these claims (Cavell, 1981, p.18). We can link this ambition to the permanent concern, in OLP and Cavell's work, to felicitous and infelicitous expression, and the vulnerability of speech. Cavell shows how film is the privileged medium for its capacity to place before us vulnerability and exposure as well as empowerment and assertion—the expressiveness of women.

> Bringing women's voices into what was then called the human conversation, would change the voice of that conversation by giving voice to aspects of human experience that were for the most unspoken or unseen. (Gilligan, 2010)

Comedies and melodrama are locales for what Cavell calls "the talent of personal expressiveness." Is this capacity, as expression of self-reliance, confined to men? The first image you meet when you open *Pursuits of Happiness* (1981) is Cary Grant (in *The Awful Truth*) "looking directly to the world with as handsome a smile as Cary Grant has it in him to give" (p. 235). This man, in the words of Emerson, carries the holiday in his eye; he is fit to stand the gaze of millions (*ibid.*).

If this is the expression of the human as transfigured by film, what kind of expression is characteristic of a woman? Cary Grant is "fit to stand the gaze of millions" because he is looking back, not "only" being looked at (*ibid.*). To "stand the gaze" is to be able to acknowledge and bear expressivity, something men and women are—differently (?)—capable of, except that this is not exactly a capability but a readiness, a capacity to attract attention, bear expression; James Stewart is described by Cavell as having a capacity for acceptance and passivity. OLP helps us to conceive moral expressivity as gendered.

What is at stake is the ability of women to achieve expression, and voice, by entering ordinary conversation, and escaping both over-expressiveness and inexpressiveness. What is at stake is emerging as a woman as subject of language.

Cavell shows how film is the privileged medium for its capacity to present us with vulnerability, exposure, and the specific expressiveness of women. Of course this account of meaning and expression is inspired by Wittgenstein's understanding of the connection of the inner to the outer (Laugier 2007a), and by Austin's attention to the powers and failures of language. Cavell's relevance for the discovery of women's voice in his work on film, his attention to women's expressiveness and capacity to hold the high ground in a conversation or a fight is grounded on a conception of voice, expression, and what Cavell describes as the threat/desire of inexpressiveness. Terror of absolute inexpressiveness, terror of absolute expressiveness, of total exposure—the polarization of inexpressiveness in two extreme states of voicelessness, connected to the fantasy of private language as criticized in Wittgenstein's *Investigations* and various writings on the philosophy of psychology, is one of the most interesting and disturbing consequences of OLP. The question is again what *the ordinary* does to philosophy and how it turns our attention to women. In this way, again, attention to *what we mean* and to our words or others' ("care for our words") defines the radicality of OLP as a resource for feminist thinking.

IV Responsibility for Ordinary Others

I will now attempt to present the ethics of care not only as attention for others, and to the ordinary work that makes our lives possible, but as an about-turn in our conceptions of responsibility, something I aimed for when I initiated French studies of care and vulnerability.

I will first present the kind of change I have tried to bring about by defending OLP and an ordinary conception of ethics and vulnerability. Then I will discuss the ethics of care as a change in conceptions of responsibility.

My work on Wittgenstein, Austin, and Cavell has meant opening new perspectives in France on the neglected question, or the theme, of the *ordinary*: early on I wanted to show the relevance of ordinary language philosophy for ethical and political issues, for example, developing an ordinary conception of politics in thinking on civil disobedience and democracy (Laugier 2004, 2010, 2014). My objective has been to open a systematic exploration of the (theoretical and practical) question of the *ordinary* on the basis of ordinary language philosophy—the "rough ground" of the uses and practices of language—by further investigating the denial or undervaluation of the ordinary in contemporary thought, and by examining concretely the forms in which this undervaluation appears in various bodies of work, mostly philosophical..

In order to do this, I am using ordinary language philosophy (OLP) as a basis for a re-definition of ethics as attention to ordinary life and care for moral expressivity and responsibility.

Ordinary others

The meaning of ordinary language philosophy does indeed lie in this recognition that language is used, spoken by a human voice. This sense of language is what the later Wittgenstein means by "form of life": the question is no longer whether language is an image of reality, but to "come back to earth" and to see the practices in which language is *caught* and which collect around our words. This makes OLP an alternative political and ethical approach, centered on the vulnerability of language.

> When we examine what we should say when, what words we should use in what situations, we are looking again not *merely* at words (or 'meanings') but also at the realities we use the words to talk about: we are using a sharpened awareness of words to sharpen our perception of, though not as the final arbiter of, the phenomena. (Austin 1962b, p. 182)

This awareness is responsibility for what we say—this tangible relation we have to our words is something that connects OLP to the general question of sensibility to words. This is how OLP led me to two main directions of thought involving gender and feminism, attention to women's voices: women's ordinary expressiveness, and the ethics of care, which was at the outset a claim for the validity of women's voice, for a different voice (Gilligan, 1982).

It is one of Austin's intuitions: we must not concern ourselves only with the analysis of what we say, but with the *we* and the *should* and the *say*. Cavell's *Must We Mean What We Say?* (1969) was the first work to ask the question of the relevance of our statements as relevance in relation to ourselves. This new (heterodox) notion of relevance is responsibility for language. The content (objective, semantic, or empirical) of propositions is no longer the question, but rather the fortunes and misfortunes of ordinary expression. What matters here then, is the search for (or loss of) the right tone or right word, conceptually, morally, socially, and sensibly. It is a matter of finding the fine sensibility to things and the adjustment of words within ordinary uses and connections. The question is: how can I know if I adequately "project" the words I have learned into new contexts? (Cavell, 1979; Laugier, 2013). There is an "unhappy" dimension, of failure in language traced by Ordinary language philosophy, which is obsessed with situations in which our words fail, are inadequate, inexpressive, inarticulate.

For Cavell, it is the question of the social contract that underwrites that of agreements in language, as is shown by the spirited analysis Rousseau offers at the opening of *The Claim of Reason* (1979). If I am representative, then I have to have a voice in the common conversation. My society, if it is an expression of me, must also allow me to find my own voice. But as Cavell went on to show, it is not at all obvious. If the others deaden my voice, speaking for me, I might still always seem to have consented. One does not have a voice, *one's own voice*, by nature: I must find my voice if I am to speak for others and they are to speak for me. For if my words are not accepted by these others, I lose my voice.

I do not know in advance how deep my agreement with myself is, how far responsibility for language may run. But if I am to have my own voice in it, I must be speaking for others, and allow others to speak for me. The alternative to speaking for myself representatively is not: speaking for myself privately. The alternative is having nothing to say, being voiceless, not even mute (Cavell, 1979, p. 28). To not be public is not to be private, it is to be *inexpressive*. Not even mute, voiceless.

From such a point of view, participating in the introduction of the ethics of care in France has been an interesting experience. I meant it as developing a heterodox ethics, inspired by approaches in moral sociology (Patricia Paperman), moral psychology (Pascale Molinier) and moral perfectionism, but above all as a matter of continuing OLP by other means—by re-centering moral philosophy on ordinary language and expressiveness. From this comes the idea of an ethics formulated *in a different voice* and expressed in a female voice.

The (polemical) importance of the ethics of care is that, just as OLP does, it subverts well-established intellectual and social hierarchies and attracts attention to a number of phenomena that are overlooked because they are connected to the female. It is a matter of showing that the (moral) sentiments of women are not an inferior level of morality, but a moral resource that has been ignored, and which would make it possible to profoundly renew moral and social thought. This is on condition of seeing care not only as a sensibility but also as an ordinary practice, an ethics defined not by abstract principles but by the concrete work done for the most part by women, and neglected because of it. In fact, taking into consideration the social, moral, and political importance of care makes it necessary to refer to "women," one of the categories to which the work of care has principally been assigned, and which has led to its being criticized as "differentialist." We can hope to defend universalism with the critique by care ethics of the incapacity of the language of justice to take into account the ordinary experiences and points of view of women as morally relevant and different. The hypothesis of a "different voice" is indeed that of a moral orientation that identifies and treats moral problems differently than the language of justice and liberal moral philosophy does.

The ethics of care has for me contributed to this transformation of ethics and voice. By proposing to valorize moral values such as caring, attention to others, solicitude, the ethics of care has changed deeply the way we look at ethics, or how ethics should look like. It has introduced ethical stakes into politics, weakening, through its critique of theories of justice, the seemingly obvious link between an ethics of justice and political liberalism. Care is a fundamental aspect of human life and consists, as Joan Tronto proposes, of "everything we do to continue, repair, and maintain ourselves so that we can live in the world as well as possible" (Tronto & Fisher, 1990, p. 41). It shows the world itself to be vulnerable.

Care corresponds to a quite ordinary reality: the fact that people look after one another, take care of one another, and thus are attentive to the functioning of the world, which depends on this kind of care. Ethics of care affirms the importance of care and attention given to others, in particular to those whose lives and wellbeing depend on particularized, continual, and daily attention: ordinary vulnerable others. Ethics of care draws our attention to the ordinary, to what we are unable to see but that is right before our eyes. An ethics that gives voice and attention to humans that are undervalued precisely because they accomplish unnoticed, invisible tasks, and take care of the basic needs of others.

This ethics is based on an analysis of the historical conditions that have favored a division of moral labor such that activities of care have been socially and morally devalorized. The assignment of women to the domestic sphere has reinforced the exclusion of these activities and preoccupations from the moral domain and the public sphere, reducing them to the rank of private sentiments devoid of moral and political import. The perspectives of care carry with them a fundamental claim concerning the importance of care for human life, for the relations that organize it, and the social and moral position of caregivers. To recognize this means recognizing that dependence and vulnerability are traits of a condition common to all, not of a special category—the vulnerable. This sort of "ordinary" realism is absent from the majority of social and moral theories, which have a tendency to reduce the activities and preoccupations of care to a concern for victims and for the weak on the part of selfless mothers. Hence the importance of acknowledging the first import of the ethics of care: *the human being is vulnerable*. So vulnerability defines ordinariness.

Care proposes bringing ethics back to the level of the "rough ground of the ordinary" (Wittgenstein, *Philosophical Investigations*), the level of everyday life. It is a practical response to specific needs, which are always those of singular others (whether close to us or not), of "the everyday life of the other"; it is work carried out just as much in the private sphere as in public; a sensibility to the details that matter. It is by giving back a (different) voice to the individual sensibility, to the intimate, that one ensures the conversation/conservation (entretien/entertaining/maintenance) of a human world.

This is obvious in the contexts of catastrophe Veena Das's *Life and Words* accounts for, when violence destroys the everyday and the very sense of *life* (2007, p. 89).

Measuring the importance of care for human life means recognizing that dependence and vulnerability are not accidents that happen only to "others." Going against the grain of the ideal of autonomy animating most moral and political theories, care reminds us that we need others in order to satisfy our primordial needs. Basing responsibility both on our connections and needs, instead of autonomy; on responsiveness and capacity to react to others, this is the redefinition of responsibility that is the basis of the ethics of care.

Responsiveness and voice

Carol Gilligan's book *In a Different Voice* (1982) was translated into French as early as 1986, only to be immediately forgotten. It may be the case that the term "*différence*" as it appears in the original French title (*Une si grande différence*) acted as a repulsive force in a country in which any difference is to be rejected on the grounds of its alleged incompatibility with the ideal of equality to which feminist theory itself is subjected. The ethics of care, as shown by polemics, hits at a sensitive point in the nexus of social and gender relations, especially in France where the main obstacle to legitimating feminism is a universalist background. Polemics about the care issue relate to a general trait of the intellectual and even academic life in France and the refusal of a revised and inclusive conception of justice.

This is a crucial, and revolutionary, point in Gilligan's work, as initiated by *In a Different Voice*. The idea that there exist female morals is so provocative, and at the same time so obvious, that its feminist origin is usually silenced. In this idea, what is asserted is that there exists another form of morals, a different voice, present in every one. The ethics of care, it should be reminded, is based on an analysis of those historical conditions that favored a division of moral labor in which care activities were socially *and* morally depreciated. That women, as is historically established, were assigned to the domestic sphere did reinforce the ejection of those activities and concerns from the public sphere, which was highly valuated by socially superior men and women. The whole domain of domestic activities has thus been surreptitiously undervalued as lacking a proper political and moral scope. The ethics of care therefore appears as contesting the legitimacy of moral, social and political philosophies in their main practice. The ethics of care, by explicitly asserting that other morals can be envisaged, opened a new field of investigation and speculation in which the two moral voices are *equal*: a morals centered on equity, impartiality and autonomy, as has been valued by a whole tradition of thought which is eventually characterized as masculine, on one hand, and on the other hand a morals articulated by a "different voice," mostly experienced by women, based on the preservation and care of human relations. This latter requires that specific situations be accounted for, hence "a mode of thought more contextual and narrative than formal and abstract." By insisting on this difference, Gilligan aimed rather at making evident our common prejudices concerning moral issues and how a different voice is silenced inside us. Gilligan's works induced a shift in moral philosophy by contesting the monopoly of abstract justice as a concept Rawls had instilled in the field of morals.

The ethics of care forces us to include in what we judge as moral, in the morals itself, in the heart of it, a voice such as Amy's. As Gilligan insisted:

> Care and caring are not women's issues; they are human concerns. And until we make explicit the gendered nature of the justice/care debate, we will continue to be mystified by its seeming intransigency. And we will not move forward in dealing with the real questions, namely, how issues of fairness and of rights intersect with issues of care and responsibility. (Gilligan, 2010)

Subverting autonomy

The reason why questions related to the ethics of care become part of the "public debate" today has to do with the crisis undergone by traditional ways of "taking care" as a result of a massive irruption of women into the labor market. In any case, whether provided within the domestic sphere or by public institutions or by the market, care is nowadays effected by women whose social status is insecure. The crisis in care affects at the same time the traditional care-givers, those whose working conditions are more and more arduous due to cuts in social benefits, and the geographical redistribution of care facilities in favor of rich countries and at the expense of poor ones.

Observing this reminds us of the importance of taking into account care and service (delegated work) simultaneously. The social (and global) division of labor related to care being as it is, we can fear that activities related to care might be divided into two parts: "emotional care," or affectionate care, an activity for white bourgeois women; and "care as a service," to be bought and delegated, dirty work to be left to subalterns. Here are the limits of any discourse valuing care: the empowerment of care-givers. The voice that ethics of care has made audible is the voice of all subalterns, all socially disadvantaged categories, ethnicized and racialized, to which the labor of care has been attributed in history.

The ethics of care makes it clear that we depend on others in a world that values autonomy so highly. The notion of care does not refer only to a type of attention to others and a set of practical activities; it also implies a sense of one's dependence and responsibility. The ethics of care does not aim at enlisting compassion and solicitude in the category of subaltern virtues dedicated to soothing an unsympathetic conception of social relations. The ethics of care aims at acknowledging a whole portion of common life systematically ignored in political discourse.

By calling for a society in which care-givers would have their voice, their relevance, and in which the tasks of care would not be structurally invisible or inconspicuous, the ethics of care brings to light the difficulty of thinking these social realities. Truly implementing care would imply both including practices linked to care in the agenda of democratic reflection and empowering those concerned—care-givers and -receivers. The recognition of the theoretical pertinence of ethics of care necessarily passes through a practical revalorization of activities linked to care and a joint modification of intellectual and political agendas, defining citizenship through bounds of care.

> The world of care, needless to say, has generally been ignored by social and political theorists. The world of care, needless to say, is often inhabited more thoroughly by women, people of lower class and caste status, working people, and other disregarded ethnic, religious, linguistic groups.

> They are the people most often excluded by politics. (Tronto, 2009, p. 15)

So care is a democratic subversion of intellectual and ethical hierarchies. The perspective of care then leads us to explore the ways in which we—in practice *and* in theory—treat the demarcation between the spheres of personal relations (familial relations, but also love, friendship) and the so-called impersonal spheres of public relations, with a hierarchy involved.

Dominant liberal ethics is, in its political articulation, the product and expression of a social practice that devalorizes both the attitude and work of care. The heterodox ethics of care gives ordinary questions—*who is taking care of whom, and how?*—the force and relevance necessary for critically examining our political and moral judgments, and understanding the narrowness of a vision of justice defined by rights.

The critical import of such questions makes *care* an issue of citizenship and democracy.

> Care is a fundamental aspect of human life. In its broadest meanings, care is complex and multidimensional: it refers both to the dispositional qualities we need to care for ourselves and others, such as being attentive to human needs and *taking responsibility* to meet such needs, as well as to the concrete work of caring. (Tronto, 2005, p. 130)

Political relations must be left open to the questioning of a wide range of ordinary human relations, such as care, trust, familiarity, responsiveness and community that are generated in globalized societies in which people who are and remain strangers are living together, and in which one can encounter people in wider circles, larger connections, the world. These relations of trust and reliance among strangers—low or weak connections—are vital to the creation of a texture of life through relational responsibility.

We need therefore to attend and tend to those horizontal networks of relations and communities that, while not being strictly speaking political, have an expressive political relevance through an acknowledgement of vulnerability and global injustice.

The notion of vulnerability indicates contexts of ordinary life in which human beings find their needs, interests, and fragilities totally exposed. Global change aggravates the exposure of human populations to disaster in industrial societies in a context of vulnerability to various and cumulated risks. The question of human security and responsibility is enhanced by the addition of vulnerabilities created by the cumulative carelessness towards humans who are invisible to us.

V Attention, Security, and the Transformation of Ethics

Even though I have been working on the concept and the ethics of care for more than ten years—so of course have encountered and discussed the concept of vulnerability, specifically the human vulnerability that is the "original condition" of the need for care, or what needs to be taken care of—I had never made clear the connection between security/safety and care before coming to Japan and, thanks to my colleagues there, met people from Fukushima and encountered the reality of Fukushima[2]. The situation in post-catastrophic Japan raises the issue of security, in a very basic and fundamental way. Such a concern translates better as "safety" than security. Security is most often seen in a positive light, for example, in the various programs that promote security (as the security of states and populations, a big thing in the Western world; security against outside "threats" that usually mean other humans. It is a conception described by Michel Foucault in his lectures at the Collège de France on "Security Territory Population" (1983) as the source of modern governmentality).

Programs about human security also aim to list positive items that would define security as preservation of basic vital interests: related to health, environment, body, sexuality, membership in a political

[2] This is a revised and short version of "Attention to Ordinary Others: Care, Vulnerability, and Human Security", *Iride*, 3/2013, dicembre, pp. 507-526. Permission by *Iride*. Many thanks to Anne Gonon and Thierry Ribault for their work and help in Japan.

community, work, and so on. The concept of security thus provides a reformulation of the capability approach, introduced by authors such as Amartya Sen (2009) and Martha Nussbaum (2011). (It is not an accident that Sen served as the President of the Commission of Human Security of UN.) But it is Sen himself who reminds us that the basic human reality is "the intense problem of human insecurity" (2003, p. 9). Our problem is then more insecurity, precarity than security, precariousness (not related etymologically to care, but sounding like it). Precarity and vulnerability are not the negative version of security, but a condition shared by (ordinary) humans and animals. The idea of security is, as Wittgenstein himself notes, almost nonsensical, and thus the basis of ethics (1923).

Ethics of care, nonsense, as a shift of paradigm in ethics

Safety (1914)

Dear! of all happy in the hour, most blest
He who has found our hid security,
Assured in the dark tides of the world that rest,
And heard our word, "Who is so safe as we?"
We have found safety with all things undying,
The winds, and morning, tears of men and mirth,
The deep night, and birds singing, and clouds flying,
And sleep, and freedom, and the autumnal earth.
We have built a house that is not for Time's throwing.
We have gained a peace unshaken by pain for ever.
War knows no power. Safe shall be my going,
Secretly armed against all death's endeavour;
Safe though all safety's lost; safe where men fall;
And if these poor limbs die, safest of all. (Rupert Brooke, 1915)

Experience of security is the deepest moral experience for Wittgenstein, who wrote his first book, the *Tractatus logico-philosophicus* (1921), under the same circumstances as Rupert Brooke, during some terrifying moments in WW1. It is interesting that both describe experiences of war and extreme danger as experience of security, more exactly, of the nonsense in the idea of security.

This chapter aims to present the ethics of care in the light of the recent necessity of a transformation of ethics. This transformation is operated from the point of view of a specific philosophical tradition, originating from Wittgenstein and ordinary language philosophy, a philosophy that calls our attention to ordinary lives by calling our attention to ordinary details of language and expression as having a moral import, and importance.

Ethical statements are not cognitive statements, and not an expression of emotions. Ethical statements are meant to struggle against the boundaries of language. I was first struck by what Wittgenstein says in the *Lecture on Ethics* (1923), after having explained in the *Tractatus logico-philosophicus* that there are no ethical statements (nonsense: do not describe any state of affairs, any reality; aim at saying, or showing something that is beyond words). Wittgenstein:

> My work consists of two parts, the one presented here plus all that I have *not* written. And it is precisely this second part that is the important point. For the ethical gets its limit drawn from the inside, as it were, by my book; ... I've managed in my book to put everything firmly into place by being silent about it .... (*ProtoTractatus*, p. 16)

Beyond, or aside from, senseless propositions, Wittgenstein identifies another group of statements which cannot carry sense: the nonsensical (*unsinnig*) propositions. Nonsense, as opposed to senselessness, is encountered when a proposition is even more radically devoid of meaning, when it transcends the bounds of sense. Under the label of *unsinnig* can be found various propositions: logical, ethical, subjective... While some nonsensical propositions are blatantly so, others seem to be meaningful—and only analysis carried out in accordance with picture theory can expose their nonsensicality. Since only what is "in" the world can be described, anything that is "higher" is excluded, including the notion of limit and the points of limit themselves. Metaphysics, and the propositions of ethics and aesthetics, which try to capture the world as a whole, are also excluded, as is the truth in solipsism, the very notion of a *subject*, for it is also not "in" the world but at its limit.

Wittgenstein makes a distinction between *saying* and *showing*. There are, beyond the senses that can be formulated in sayable (sensical) propositions, things that can only be shown. These—the logical form of the world, the pictorial form, etc.—show themselves in the form of propositions, in the symbolism and logical propositions, and even in the unsayable (metaphysical, ethical, aesthetic) statements. "What can be shown cannot be said." But it is there, in language, even though it cannot be said.

Wittgenstein illustrates this idea with the experience of feeling absolutely safe. I mean the state of mind in which one is inclined to say "I am safe, nothing can injure me whatever happens."

> Now the same applies to the experience of absolute safety. We all know what it means in ordinary life to be safe. I am safe in my room, when I cannot be run over by an omnibus. I am safe if I have had whooping cough and cannot therefore get it again. To be safe essentially means that it is physically impossible that certain things should happen to me and therefore it is nonsense to say that I am safe whatever happens. Again this is a misuse of the word 'safe' as the other example was of a misuse of the word 'existence' or 'wondering.' (…)
>
> That is to say: I see now that these nonsensical expressions were not nonsensical because I had not yet found the correct expressions, but that their nonsensicality was their very essence. For all I wanted to do with them was just to go beyond the world and that is to say beyond significant language. My whole tendency and, I believe, the tendency of all men who ever tried to write or talk ethics or religion was to run against the boundaries of language.
>
> This running against the walls of our cage is perfectly, absolutely hopeless. Ethics so far as it springs from the desire to say something about the ultimate meaning of life, the absolute good, the absolute valuable, can be no science. What it says does not add to our knowledge in any sense. But it is a document of a tendency in the human mind which I personally cannot help respecting deeply and I would not for my life ridicule it. (*Lecture on Ethics*, last §)

Here nonsense is the only way to express what is essential to the idea of safety: "Safe though all safety's lost"; to understand this sentence would be to understand something very deep in any experience of absolute safety, that is, absolute unsecurity—a threat to human existence, and to the human.

To show the stakes of this relocation of safety I want now to connect it to a redefinition of ethics, and of moral life that has been proposed by Cora Diamond (1991) and by Stanley Cavell (1979), as refocused on ordinary lives. The main point here is that depicting our ordinary lives does not mean simply describing our practices. Ethics cannot be described by reference to our customs, and our practices cannot form a foundation for ethics. Ethics is not empirical in this sense. This is connected with Diamond's saying that our practices are *exploratory* and not merely given. The point is not so much to argue as to explore, to change the way we see things. Our practice is itself shaped by what we expect from ethics, and ethics itself is shaped both by what we do, and by what we want or imagine. Our practices cannot form a foundation for ethics. But ethics is not a set of principles to be edicted and argued, then applied to human reality.

There is, for Diamond, no subject matter specific to ethics. This might seem to make ethics more general, but it does just the opposite: Diamond's aim, drawing on Wittgenstein, is to define an ethics of (attention to) the particular.

> Just as logic is not, for Wittgenstein, a particular subject, with its own body of truths, but penetrates all thought, so ethics has no particular subject matter; rather, an ethical spirit, an attitude to the world and life, can penetrate any thought and talk. So the contrast I want is that between ethics conceived as a sphere of discourse among others in contrast with ethics tied to everything there is or can be, the world as a whole, life. (Diamond, 2000, p. 153)

If there is a point in wanting to go back to "our practices." it lies in examining this heterogeneous ensemble of linguistic practices, what we say at the heart of the whirl of our forms of life, our form of life (or better, our life form) in language. Realism in ethics, from this view, consists in returning to ordinary language, in examining our words and paying attention to them, in taking care of them (taking care of our words and expressions, and of the ordinary others').

Diamond critiques a fascination in ethics comparable to that of Frege and Russell in logic, a fascination with an ideal of rationality that can "ground all moral arguments" (Diamond, 2000). But not everything in ethics happens by way of arguments. We imagine, like Frege, that "it would be impossible for geometry to formulate precise laws if it used strings as lines and knots in the strings as points." In the same way, we believe that ethics cannot be practiced without the idea of a norm and of an "ethical must" that are quite separate from ordinary reality with its strings and knots—the warp and weft of our life that Wittgenstein evokes in various places (Wittgenstein, *Remarks on the Philosophy Psychology II*, §862). This is the realistic spirit: seeing that what matters, what needs attending to, is the knots and strings, the weave of our ordinary lives.

Details define what has to come to our attention (the motifs or patterns). We could analyze the way Wittgenstein aims at ethical "exploration" of the human life form. Here we can use Wittgenstein's idea again, repeatedly quoted by Cavell, of human beings' agreement *in* language, *in* a life form.

> It is what human beings say that is true or false, and they agree in the language that they use. That is not agreement in opinions but in form of life. (Wittgenstein, *Philosophical Investigations*, p. 241-242)

Truth and falsity, for Wittgenstein, are to be defined in connection with this background.

> How could human behavior be described? Surely only by showing the actions of a variety of humans as they are all mixed up together. Not what *one* man is doing *now*, but the whole hurly-burly, is the background against which we see an action. (*Remarks on the Philosophy of Psychology II*)

This is why, as Hilary Putnam said, our ethical lives cannot be captured with a half a dozen words like "good," "right," "duty," "fairness," "justice," and the like (Putnam 2004, p. 106-107), but call for an exploration of the way our ethical preoccupations are embedded in our language and our life, in a cluster of words that extends beyond our ethical vocabulary itself and sustains complex connections with a variety of institutions and practices. In order to describe ethical understanding we should have to describe all of this, all these particular uses of words, of which a general definition cannot be given.

This notion of *human behavior* is connected to Wittgenstein's idea of a form of life/life form (a form taken by life, as Cavell and some anthropologists say), which also defines a texture. "Texture" thus refers to an unstable reality that cannot be fixed by concepts, or by determinate particular objects, but only by the recognition of gestures, manners, and styles. A form of life, from the point of view of ethics, can be grasped only by attention to textures or moral patterns, perceived as "morally expressive" in/against the background provided by a form of life.

Our capacity for moral expression is rooted in a mutable form of life, vulnerable to our better and worse uses of language. It is the form of life that determines the ethical structure of expression, which itself, on the other hand, acts back upon the form of life and gives it form. The type of interest, the care that we have for others, the importance that we give them, does not exist except in the possibility of the revelation of the self in its moral expression.

What is at stake here is the validity of general moral principles, hence, the relationship between the general and the particular. By bringing ethics back to the "rough ground of the ordinary" (Wittgenstein), the level of everyday life, care aims at a practical response to specific needs, which are always those of singular ordinary others..

Care as a particularist ethics

A basis of the ethics of care is particularism. Not only attention to the particular other, but a principle of immanence that is a turn in moral thought: against what Wittgenstein in the *Blue Book* (1958) called the "craving for generality"—the desire to pronounce general rules of thought and action to be applied top-down. It is the attempt to describe and valorize, within morality, attention to the particular(s), to the ordinary neglected detail of human life. So here we have an actual bottom-up conception of ethics (except that it still remained to be asked why the top is the top etc.) Analyses in terms of care are inscribed within a critique of standard moral theory, which claims the primacy of the description of actual moral practices in ethical reflection.

Practical ethics of care starts from concrete moral problems and observes how we cope—not in order to abstract from these particular solutions (which would be to fall back into the craving for generality), but in order to perceive the value of (in) the particular. Conceiving morality on the model of justice and rights (a strong tendency in moral thought) leads to neglecting some of the most important aspects of moral life—our proximities, our motivations, our relations—in favor of concepts that are far removed from our ordinary questionings and uses of language, disembedded from our everyday lives: such as obligation, rationality, choice. Qualities such as generosity, or kindness, seem to evade available moral theories' capacities for description or appreciation. Focusing on notions of rational action or moral choice leaves out an important part of ordinary moral questioning and activities.

When Diamond affirms, in her introduction to *The Realistic Spirit* (1991, p. 23-24), that moral philosophy has largely become "stupid and insensitive," she means insensitive to the human specificity of moral questioning, to this ordinary moral life bound up with others. For her, this is a matter of sensitivity to what is said and to expression and would include those particular situations in which one just cannot stand a certain attitude, or a certain vocabulary; when one no longer wants to argue, but asks oneself, "Who is this person, in what world does he or she live? Within what life, what world can our discussion take place?" (Diamond, 1991, Introduction II). Again, the idea of nonsense and nonsensicality open the way to a comprehension of ethics.

Carol Gilligan (1982) pointed out, in Kohlberg's model of moral development, the inability of the language of justice to take into account as morally pertinent the experiences and points of view of women: she hypothesized the "different voice" of a moral orientation that would identify and treat moral problems differently than the language of justice. This different orientation would have a coherence and validity of its own, which the language of care would allow one to grasp.

A properly political, and not only moral, stake of care is introducing a political dimension into family relations, into the private—into the intimate, where claims for equality seem inadequate. Care allows for taking into account the particularity of thc relations of proximity that form within the family, and for re-examining the familial universe as an arena within which relations are shaped by tensions between justice and care. The perspective of care then leads us to explore the ways in which we—in practice *and* in theory—treat the demarcation between the spheres of personal relations (familial relations, but also love, friendship) and the so-called impersonal spheres of public relations, with of course a hierarchy involved: so the political stakes in the ethics of care are again the ethical enablement of populations and categories that are assumed as being morally inferior.

Viewing care as socially, morally and politically important thus implies a reference to "women" as a category to which the labor associated with care has been specifically restricted and assigned. Since speaking of "women" means introducing a category (as is any theory assuming that such a category does exist), Gilligan's approach was dismissed as "essentialist." The ethics of care is, however, a claim for more realism, in the sense given to this word in Cora Diamond's *The Realistic Spirit* (1991), meaning the necessity to see what liesright under one's eyes: the reality of inequalities. If something like morals exists, it can be seen not in a set of preexisting numerable rules nor in a moral reality but in the mere immanence of situations, affects and practices. No "care" without the expression of everyone's voice: here lies the *importance* of a different voice. What Gilligan did establish was that the language of justice cannot account for the pertinence of women's experiences and points of view—these experiences and the moral perspectives they produce being disqualified as deficient or marginal. If the possibility that women might be morally deficient is excluded, then the hypotheses that there exists a "different voice" must be taken seriously, along with that of a moral orientation identifying and treating moral problems in another way, different from that implied by the language of justice. Analyses of things in terms of care are devoted to such an objective of articulation and clarification.

Gilligan has clearly shown the generality of her approach: justice and care are two different tonalities, or rival voices, existing inside each of us, the care voice being less inhibited in girls than in boys. The notion of "care," in as much as it covers very practical activities and a form of sensitivity, a sustained attention to others and a sense of responsibility and dependence, breaks with theories of impartial justice.

The reason why questions related to the ethics of care become part of the "public debate" today has to do with the crisis undergone by traditional ways of "taking care" due to a massive irruption of women into the labor market. In any case, whether provided in the domestic sphere or by public institutions or by the market, care is nowadays performed by women whose social status is insecure: nurses, girls helping at home, social workers, etc., not to mention all these jobs related to care that are all the more devaluated in so far as they are being occupied by women, like teachers, doctors, etc. The crisis in care and the care drain affect at the same time the traditional care-givers, those whose working conditions are more and more arduous due to cutbacks in social support and the geographical redistribution of care facilities, in favor of rich countries and at the expense of poor ones. The social (and global) division of labor related to care being as it is, activities related to care might be divided into two parts: "emotional care"—affectionate care given to particular others—an activity for white bourgeois women; and "care as a service," to be bought and delegated, dirty work to be left to subalterns. The generalization of the concept of vulnerability may thus be questioned. Almost nobody would choose to provide that second (devalued) kind of care if he (or she) can avoid it; certainly not the intellectuals who praise a caring society and emotional work without bothering *who* is going to provide the kind of care that they claim to be a right due to (rich) citizens. One should question the meaning of a vulnerability everybody ought to feel as a care-receiver, but often denies to care-givers. These are questions that have not yet reached the level of public debate. The voice that ethics of care has made audible is not only women's voice; it is the voice of all subalterns, all socially disadvantaged categories, ethnicized and racialized, to which the labor of care has been attributed.

> The issue of care today is made more urgent by the crisis of care, and the global injustice of global poverty: by focusing on and valuing care in the North, we insulate people in the North from the harm their actions inflict upon others. Ordinary citizens in the Anglo-American world, says Tronto, lack determinate knowledge about their complicity in global poverty. "They do not see global poverty and inequality as morally important issues for us." (Tronto, 2012, p. 312).

Sociologist Kari Norgaard reported as early as 2006 on the ways in which Norwegians, well aware of the problem, declined to participate in a social movement aimed at addressing global warming. When asked why she did not do more, one of her informants responded, "People want to protect themselves a little bit" (Norgaard, 2006, p. 357). Today, Greta Thunberg reminds us all about the dangers of such a selfish attitude.

Such protection, just like the "security" promoted in the Western world, is one-sided. So there is a strong connection between care and global justice, a connection that seems to void the classical care/justice debate, for only the care perspective enables us to properly take care of the problem of global injustice. The main inequalities, today, are in the area of care.

Even if it is difficult to believe in the solutions promoted by Sen to support the cause of greater human security in the world—"protection" (when people are too vulnerable) and "empowerment" (when people, with the help of each other, can enhance their ability to withstand threatening developments), more or less: "our ability to look after ourselves and others"— his objective, the disconnection of citizenship and possession of rights in favor of a citizenship based on vulnerability, is probably the main challenge, in dark times, for a new and democratic Enlightenment. A new version of cosmopolitanism, or citizenship of the world, not to be asked for, conquered, or claimed, but acknowledged as a reality.

VI Care as Subversion

Carol Gilligan's book, *In a Different Voice* (1982), a best-seller in United States, was translated into French as early as 1986, only to be forgotten immediately. It may be the case that the term "*différence*" as it appears in the original French title (*Une si grande différence*, 1986) acted as a repellent force in a country where any difference is to be rejected on the grounds of its alleged incompatibility with the ideal of equality to which feminist theory itself is subjected. Yet today, a generation later, nothing has really changed and the controversy about the care issue has not evolved at all. In France, the usual objection to the ethics of care holds that, far from belonging to feminist theory, it tends to make the distinction between men and women more rigid and essential in character by the reference to a moral content: women, in this view, represent attention to others, especially close others. while men emblematize autonomy and impartiality; women are supposed to be associated with domestic activities while men take part in active life; women are private while men belong to public life. The ethics of care,[3] by emphasizing the social, moral and public importance of qualities such as attention to others and caring activities, would only reinstate and confirm stereotypic views. Such a polemic can be viewed as an example of how the French

[3] "L'éthique du *care*" in the original. Although "care" in its ordinary meaning may be translated by "soin," the word "care" is kept untranslated in the French discussions on the ethics of care, to account for all the dimensions of attention/activity/work encapsuled in the name/verb care.

male-dominated political and/or academic world usually reacts to issues related to feminism: by opposing a "correct" version of feminism, a legitimate and true one, to minor ones—a process academics are happy to encourage by providing arguments for politicians. The ethics of care were accused of indulging in a caricatural view of 'femininity' and several attacks against 'le care' in France. For instance, Michel Onfray, in an op-ed in *Le Monde* (2010, June 12), advised "women" that they should re-read their "classics" (for example, Beauvoir, a "good" feminist). Similarly, officially established feminists, who are used to manipulating ambient misogyny, advocated against the ethics of care, viewed by them as "maternal"; while the few women in government took a stand against the ethics of care, claiming to be defending republican equality; not to mention the ironic and demagogic tone adopted by people at the left alluding to a "care society." (Laugier, 2010, June 20; 2010, April 21)

The ethics of care hits at a sensitive point in the nexus of social and gender relations, especially in France, where the main obstacle to legitimating feminism is a universalist background along with its differentialist companion. Polemics about the care issue relate to a general trait of the intellectual and even academic life in France, where a big difference can be observed between the quality of social and generally speaking critical thought and its lack of development when it comes to feminist matters. Objections to the ethics of care, as they are voiced in that specific space at the intersection of intellectual and political worlds, only serve to display a national weakness in public feminist thought exemplified by the low level of credibility attributed to research in the field. Criticism of the care issue expresses only the contempt in which a whole field of human activity is held in our society, even among women. A further instance of a situation in which academic researches are validated or devaluated according to the value attached to their object.

Subverting morals

An important spin-off from the ethics of care is that morals have become plural. This is a crucial, and most revolutionary, point in

Gilligan's work, as initiated in *In a Different Voice* (1982) and pursued in *The Deepening Darkness* (2008). The idea that feminine morals exist is so provocative, and at the same time so obvious, that its feminist origin is usually silenced. By this idea, what is asserted is that there exists another form of morals, a different voice, present in every one; this voice is neglected precisely because, in the first place and from an empiricist point of view, it is the voice of women referring to activities that appear as feminine because they are usually restricted to women. The ethics of care, it should be reminded, is based on an analysis of those historical conditions that favored a division of moral labor in which care activities were socially *and* morally depreciated. The fact that women, as has been historically established, were assigned to the domestic sphere, served to reinforce the rejection of those activities and concerns from the public sphere, which was highly valuated by socially superior men and women. The whole domain of domestic activities has thus been surreptitiously undervalued as lacking a proper political and moral scope. The ethics of care therefore appears as contesting the legitimacy of moral, social and political philosophies in their main practice.

The ethics of care, by explicitly asserting that other morals can be envisaged, opened a new field of investigation and speculation in which the two moral voices are *on a par*: a morals centered on equity, impartiality and autonomy, as has been valued by a whole tradition of thought which is eventually characterized as masculine, on one hand; a morals articulated by a "different voice," mostly experienced by women, based on the preservation and care of human relations, on the other hand. This latter requires that specific situations be accounted for; it requires, in Gilligan's words, "a mode of thought more contextual and narrative than formal and abstract" (1982, p. 28). By insisting on this difference, Carol Gilligan did not intend to introduce an essential difference; she aimed rather at making evident our common prejudices concerning moral issues and how a different voice is silenced inside all of us. Gilligan's works induced a shift in moral philosophy by contesting the monopoly of justice as a concept John Rawls had instilled in the field of morals.

The different-voice revolution occurs when Gilligan introduces Amy into ethics. Amy is a girl aged eleven. She is confronted, along with a boy, Jake, of about the same age, with the so-called Heinz's dilemma: either steal the medicine badly needed by Heinz's dying wife or let her die. According to Jake, Heinz should steal the drug: saving his wife's life must be given first priority; therefore he is *entitled* to commit robbery. Amy's answer to the dilemma is different, suggesting that there might be other alernatives, without a robbery; Heinz might borrow money, for instance. Moreover, what use is it to Heinz's wife, she argues, if he goes to jail? Heinz must not commit robbery and his wife must not die. Amy suggests that Heinz and his wife talk to each other to find a solution. Jake and Amy are representative, respectively, of the view according to ethics of justice and the perspective of the ethics of care. Amy's moral judgment relies on attention being paid to all specificities of the problem. Her world view is made up of interwoven human relations, the thread of which builds a coherent whole, and not of isolated independent individuals whose relations are governed by systems of rules. From the dominant ethical point of view, the moral value of Amy's thinking is *less* than Jake's—even zero. The ethics of care is revolutionary in the sense that it forces us to include what we judge as moral, in the morals themselves, at their heart, a voice such as Amy's. The ethics of care claims that the two voices, Amy's and Jake's, should have equal status. Amy's voice, because it sounds (briefly or permanently) in each of us—man and woman—represents such a provocative claim.

Subverting politics

The concept of care, as one of critical politics, questions the true meaning to be accorded to morals and politics when grasped by a specific position. Carole Pateman addressed this difficult issue some years after Gilligan and in a different direction, in a book whose title speaks for itself: *The Sexual Contract* (1988). Pateman radicalizes and politicizes the idea that is at the basis of the ethics of care, namely that predominant ethics, with their articulation to politics, and more specifically to past and present theories of "contract," are produced by and express the very idea of "patriarchy," which uses them as tools in submitting women to its power. Similarly, ethics and politics, as they appear in philosophical speculations, are mere translations of social practice in its devaluation of labor and attitudes related to the idea of care, thus restricting the corresponding jobs to women, poor people and migrants in priority.

Viewing care as socially, morally and politically important thus implies a reference to "women" as a category to which the labor associated with care has been specifically confined and assigned. Since speaking of "women" means introducing a suspect category (as is any theory assuming that such a category does exist), Gilligan's approach was easily considered "essentialist." The mere immediacy of such a characterization in the French context does in itself point to the existence of prejudices impeaching any critical thought on the predominant character of the common view on morals. Referring to universality, a common and constant practice in France, results, as Christine Delphy (2010) has repeatedly emphasized, in omitting that universalism is a project, not a reality, therefore denying gender inequalities. The ethics of care brings us back to such a claim for more realism, in the sense given to this word in Cora Diamond's *The Realistic Spirit* (1991), meaning the necessity to see what lies just under one's eyes: the reality of inequalities. Reflections on care bring morals back to their proper domain, that is to say our practice, just as Wittgenstein wants to bring words from their metaphysical use to their daily use, where they do *mean* something to us. If something like morals exists, it can be seen not in a set of pre-existing numerable rules nor in a moral reality but in the mere immanence of situations, affects and practices. No "care" without the expression of everyone's voice: here lies the *importance* of a different voice. What Gilligan did establish was that the language of justice cannot account for the pertinence of women's experiences and points of view—the experiences and the moral perspectives they produce being disqualified as deficient or marginal. If the possibility that women might be morally deficient is excluded, then the hypothesis that there exists a "different voice" must be taken seriously, along with that of a moral orientation identifying and treating moral problems in another way, different from that implied by the language of justice. Analyses of things in terms of care are devoted to such an objective of articulation and clarification.

One should now ask the question: how is it that Gilligan's approach has been considered "essentialist"? Gilligan has clearly shown the generality of her approach: justice and care are two different tonalities, or rival voices, existing in each of us, the care voice being less inhibited in girls than in boys. As Gilligan insisted in a recent lecture:

> Care and caring are not women's issues; they are human concerns. And until we make explicit the gendered nature of the justice/care debate–we will continue to be mystified by its seeming intransigency. And we will not move forward in dealing with the real questions, namely, how issues of fairness and of rights intersect with issues of care and responsibility. (2010)

The notion of care, in as much as it covers very practical activities and a form of sensitivity, a sustained attention to others and a sense of responsibility and dependence, breaks with theories of impartial justice. The theory of care does not aim at instilling pity, compassion, solicitude and benevolence as subsidiary values that would lessen the harshness of a cold conception of social relations, an impartial conception of justice based on the primacy of rights attributed to autonomous, separated, rational individuals. Such a description would better suit what is called solicitude, that is to say, care from the perspective of justice or as it appears in that political discourse whose target it has been since its appearance.

Subverting feminism

In France, the diagnosis as far as feminism is concerned is that of delayed development, mainly due to the backwardness of the intellectual class. In other words, the state of delayed development of French feminism is the form adopted by male domination in the intellectual field. Mocking American theories for their excesses is common among French male and female academics, who insist on the alleged differentialism of American thought. A feature to which France would bravely oppose such national principles as fraternity, equality and universality. These notions systematically asserted in discussions on the care issue are viewed as being of a superior kind, to which any feminist thesis should be submitted, without any critical reflection referring to their masculine wording ("fraternity"). This could explain why, in the conventional discourse on "*soin*" and "*sollicitude*" that attempts to replace the ethics of care in the contemporary controversy, any reference to the feminist dimension of the problem is systematically repressed. The debate about the care issue probably appears in some quarters as the long expected opportunity for attacking feminism through feminism itself. There is nothing new in this maneuver, which consists in eroding the radical aspect of the notion of care and buffing its novelty by reformulating it in familiar terms. As in assertions such as these: since the care issue has already been taken into account through the idea of solidarity without any reference to any feminist perspective, it is no use introducing this perspective into the problem; or, a doctrine such as the ethics of care, overloaded as it is with "feelings" originating in the restricted space of family, can only be of minor theoretical value when compared with theories related to "real," "true," major ethical and political problems, those that are taken into account in public life.

Critics of the ethics of care rely on a misinterpretation of the idea of care, thought of as allegedly referring to that other idea that women's natural position is one of sacrifice and abnegation. The ethics of care precisely excludes this sort of essentialist view. It is ironic that the ethics of care can be accused of not asserting what it has been really asserted from the beginning, namely equality. Real and true equality, not that theoretical equality that goes with citizenship, for instance. The ethics of care is subverting the predominant way of addressing two important complementary issues: civic equality (women are equal to men by definition of their common status of "*citoyen français*" (French citizen); therefore claiming specific rights for women is pointless, since women already have those rights); and the so-called "*mérite républicain*" (every citizen of the Republic should be treated according to his or her merits—meaning that women should not be favored as such; no quotas, no positive discrimination, since it would go against equal rights for all). As many feminists have asserted, but none so empirically established as Gilligan's analyses have shown, criteria defining what is right or wrong, what should be valued or discarded (criteria for morals and quality), appear under the guise of universalism while they are in fact those of a patriarchal society; they are masculine criteria in the sense that the values they promote are those forged by masculine domination in order to ensure this domination. Gilligan's strength lies in her moral epistemology, in exhibiting how gender oriented our judgments are when it comes to morals, value and intellectual matters. The ethics of care thus brings feminism back to its origin: equality. One of the problems we have to face in France—the issue is that of inequality among women—is how universalism serves as an argument and a pretext, in order to make feminism compatible with social contempt (I could do it by myself, on my own, why can't others do the same?). This argument underlies all sorts of stances (against quotas, against positive discrimination, etc.) often taken by women themselves. As a matter of fact, the question raised by the ethics of care is that unpleasant one of inequalities among women: how to acknowledge it? How to analyze it? Once more, the ethics of care serves to reveal an occulted question. The autonomy gained by some women—those who speak in the name of women—through work and through the increased possibilities to have children taken care of, was obtained in a masculine way, if I may say so. I mean that this autonomy was gained not by a transfer of domestic charges in the direction of men, nor by sharing them equally, but by putting other women to work, at the service of women. I am not going to indulge in easy ironical words about women who have become employers, all the more so since they still have the moral and administrative burden of employing someone at home. I'd rather insist on the fact that once more we have to look at what is just under our eyes: tasks related to care, traditionally handled by women, still exist, even if in our privileged western countries they are handled by others, in as much as we can afford it. The fact that these tasks are undertaken by immigrants just adds to the moral devaluation of the idea of "care."

The reason why questions related to the ethics of care become part of the public debate today has to do with the crisis undergone by traditional ways of "taking care" as result of a massive irruption of women into the labor market. In any case, whether provided in the domestic sphere or by public institutions or by the market, care is nowadays performed by women whose social status is still insecure: nurses, girls helping at home, social workers, etc., not to mention the jobs related to care that are all the more devaluated because they are being done by women such as teachers, doctors, etc. The crisis in care at the same time affects traditional care-givers who work more since they live longer, those whose working conditions are increasingly arduous due to cutbacks in social funding and the geographical redistribution of care facilities in favor of rich countries and to the expense of poor ones (see Paperman & Laugier, 2005; Glenn, 2009).

This is reminds us of the importance of simultaneously taking into account care and service (delegated work): "service," or rather "servitude," as Geneviève Fraisse explains in her book *Femmes toutes mains* (1979, 2009). The social (and global) division of labor related to care being as it is, activities related to care might be divided in two parts: "emotional care", affectionate care given to particular others, an activity for white bourgeois women; and "care as a service," to be bought and delegated, dirty work to be left to subalterns.

Here are the limits of any discourse valuing care: the empowerment of caregivers. Almost nobody would choose to give that second kind of care if he (or she) could avoid it; certainly not the politicians and intellectuals who praise a "*société du soin*" (a caring society) without bothering *who* is going to give, organize and fund the kind of care that they claim to be rightfully due to (French) citizens. One should question the meaning of a vulnerability that everybody feels as a care-receiver but refuses to acknowledge in care-givers. These are questions that have never reached the level of public debate; at stake are not just care and protection as such, but politics. The voice that ethics of care has made audible is not only women's voice; it is the voice of all subalterns, all socially disadvantaged categories, ethnicized and racialized, to which the labor of care has been attributed throughout history.

The ethics of care makes it clear that we depend on others in a world that values autonomy so highly. The notion of care does not refer only to a type of attention to others and a set of practical activities; it also implies a sense of one's dependence and responsibility. The ethics of care does not aim at enlisting compassion and solicitude in the category of subordinate virtues dedicated to soothing an unsympathetic conception of social relations, or (which amounts to the same) instilling domination under cover of protection. The ethics of care aims at the acknowledgment of a whole portion of common life systematically ignored in political discourse. Care is what makes a common life possible. Joan Tronto and Berenice Fisher suggest that care should be defined at the most general level as a generic activity meaning everything we do in order to perpetuate and repair our "world," so that we can live in it as well as it possible. This "world" includes our bodies, our environment, and ourselves as elements we try to assemble into a complex and life-sustaining network.

This could help us see care ethics not as an "essentialist" move in ethics but as an ethics that gives expression to humans who are undervalued because they accomplish unnoticed, invisible tasks. The ethics of care merges with this realistic spirit by drawing our attention to the place of ordinary words in the weave and details of our lives, and our relation to, and distance from, our words. This connection between care and what counts has been highlighted by Harry Frankfurt in *The Importance of What We Care About* (1988) and by Cavell about film criticism.

> The moral I draw is this: the question what becomes of objects when they are filmed and screened has only one source of data for its answer, namely the appearance and significance of just these objects and people that are in fact to be found in the succession of films, or passages of films, that matter to us. To express their appearances, and define those significances, and articulate the nature of this mattering, are acts that help to constitute what we might call film criticism. (Cavell, 1984, p. 183)

Importance lies in the details, and this particularism of attention to detail is another connection of OLP to care. Feminist moral philosophy displaces its very field of study, its point, from general concepts to the examination of particular visions, of individuals' "configurations" of thought—forms of life, textures of being.

This is obvious when one coansiders the place Cavell assigns to Hollywood film in the creation of a woman, and the emergence of a generation of women and women's voices. Women needed—need—"more than rights" (as Annette Baier calls it: more than justice): equality of voice, which comes from a fuller expression: so conversational equality, speech equality in general. The women/actresses in films (for example, Katharine Hepburn, Irene Dunne, Barbara Stanwyck) represent a generation of women capable of giving expression to these claims for equality (Cavell 1981, p. 18).

We can connect this ambition to the permanent concern, in OLP, with felicitous and infelicitous expression, and the vulnerability of speech. Cavell shows how film is the privileged medium for vulnerability and exposure, but also empowerment and assertion—expressiveness of women as sought by Gilligan. No care without the expression of everyone's voice: here lies the *importance* of the different voice.

Cavell shows the capacity of the cinema to put before us the expressiveness of women (1984). This account of meaning and expression intensifies Wittgenstein's and Austin's attention to the powers and failures of language. Cavell's and Das's relevance for the discovery of women's voice, his attention to women's expressiveness and capacity to hold the high ground in a conversation, or a fight, is grounded in a conception of voice and what Cavell (1984) describes as the threat/desire of inexpressiveness—fear of inexpressiveness, vs. terror of expressiveness, of total exposure—the polarization of inexpressiveness into two states of voicelessness, which is the concrete meaning of the fantasy of private language as criticized in Wittgenstein's *Investigations* and of what Das calls, after Cavell, skepticism.

Bibliography

Agee J. (2013) *Cotton Tenants: Three Families*. New York: Melville House Publishing.

Alsaleh C. & Laugier S. (Eds.). (2011). *J.L. Austin et la philosophie du langage ordinaire*. Olms: Hildesheim.

Anscombe G.E.M. (1958). Modern Moral Philosophy. *Philosophy*, *33*(124), pp. 1-19.

Austin J.L. (1962a). *How to Do Things with Words*. Oxford: Oxford University Press.

Austin J. L. (1962b). *Philosophical Papers*. Oxford: Oxford University Press.

Austin J. L. (1964). *Sense and Sensibilia*. Oxford: Oxford University Press.

Baier A. (1985). *Postures of the Mind: Essays on Mind and Morals*. Minneapolis: University of Minnesota Press.

Baier A. (1995). What do Women Want in a Moral Theory? In Baier A. (Ed.), *Moral Prejudices: Essays on Ethics*. Cambridge: Harvard University Press.

Baz A. (2011). *When Words are Called For: A Defense of Ordinary Language Philosophy*. Cambridge: Harvard University Press.

Bourdieu P. (1990). *In Other Words: Essays Towards a Reflexive Sociology, transl. Adamson* M. Stanford: Stanford University Press.

Brooke R. (1915). *1914 and other Poems*. London: Sidgwick & Jackson.

Cavell, S. (1969). *Must We Mean What We Say?* Cambridge: Cambridge University Press.

Cavell S. (1971). *The World Viewed.* Cambridge: Harvard University Press.

Cavell S. (1979). *The Claim of Reason: Wittgenstein, Skepticism, Morality and Tragedy*. Oxford: Oxford University Press.

Cavell S. (1981). *Pursuits of Happiness: The Hollywood Comedy of Remarriage*. Cambridge: Harvard University Press.

Cavell S. (1984). *Themes Out of School: Effects and Causes*. Chicago: The University of Chicago Press.

Cavell, S. (1989). *This New Yet Unapproachable America.* Albuquerque: Living Batch Press.

Cavell, S. (1996). A *Pitch of Philosophy. Autobiographical Exercises*. Cambridge: Harvard University Press.

Cavell S. (2003). *Emerson's Transcendental Etudes*. Hodge D. J. (Ed.). Stanford: Stanford University Press.

Cavell S. (2007). Preface. In Das V. *Life and Words*. Stanford: Stanford University Press.
Cavell, S. (2009). *Dire et vouloir dire*, tr. Laugier S. & Fournier C. Paris: Le Cerf.
Cavell S. (2010). *Little Did I Know, Excerpts of Memory*. Stanford: Stanford University Press.
Crary A. (2007). *Beyond Moral Judgment*. Cambridge: Harvard University Press.
Das V. (2007). *Life and Words*. Violence and the descent into everyday life. Stanford: Stanford University Press.
Das V. (2015). *Affliction. Health, Disease, Poverty*. New York: Fordham University Press.
Das V. (2020). *Textures of the Ordinary. Doing Anthropology after Wittgenstein*. New York: Fordham University Press.
Delphy C. (2010). *Un universalisme si particulier*. Paris: Syllepse.
Diamond C. (1988). Losing Your Concepts Ethics 98:2 pp. 273–4.
Diamond C. (1991). *The Realistic Spirit: Wittgenstein, Philosophy, and the Mind*. Cambridge: MIT Press.
Diamond C. (1997). Moral Differences and Distances: Some Questions. In Alanen L., Heinamaa S. & Wallgren T. (Eds.), *Commonality and Particularity in Ethics* (pp. 197-234). London: Macmillan.
Diamond C. (2000). Ethics, imagination and the method of Wittgenstein's Tractatus. In Crary A. & Read R. J. (Eds.), *The New Wittgenstein* (pp. 149-173). London: Routledge.
Emerson Ralph Waldo (1977). Experience, in *Essays, Second Series*, The Library of America.
Foucault M. (1978 [2004]). La philosophie analytique de la politique. In *Dits et écrits, tome 3* (pp. 536-553). Paris: Gallimard.
Foucault M. (1983). *Sécurité, Territoire, Population. Cours au Collège de France 1977-1978*. Paris: Gallimard & Du Seuil.
Fraisse G. (1979). *Femmes toutes mains. Un essai sur le service domestique*. Paris: Le Seuil.
Fraisse G. (2009). *Service et servitude. Essai sur les femmes toutes mains*. Lormont: Le Bord de l'eau.
Frankfurt H. (1988). *The Importance of What We Care About*. Cambridge: Cambridge University Press.
Gautier C. & Laugier S. (Eds.). (2006). *L'ordinaire et le politique*. Paris: Presses universitaires de France.
Gilligan C. (1982). *In a Different Voice*. Cambridge: Harvard University Press.
Gilligan C. (1995). Moral orientation and development. In Held V. (Ed.) *Justice and Care: Essential Readings in Feminist Ethics* (pp. 31-46). Boulder: Westview Press.
Gilligan C. (2010). *In a Different Voice: Looking Back to Look Forward*. Unpublished lecture, Paris.
Gilligan C. & Richards D. (2008). *The Deepening Darkness: Patriarchy, Resistance, and Democracy's Future*. Cambridge: Cambridge University Press.

Glenn E. N. (2009). Le travail forcé : citoyenneté, obligation statutaire et assignation des femmes au care. In Molinier P., Laugier S. & Paperman P. (Eds.), *Qu'est-ce que le care? Souci des autres, sensibilité, responsabilité* (pp. 113-131). Paris: Payot.

Goffman E. (1969). The Insanity of Place. *Psychiatry, 32*(4), pp. 357-388.

Goffman E. (1974). *Frame Analysis: An Essay on the Organization of Experience*. New York: Harper & Row.

Goffman E. (1987). *Forms of Talk*. Philadelphia: University of Pennsylvania Press.

Goffman E. (2005). *Interaction Ritual: Essays in Face to Face Behavior*. New Jersey: Transaction Publishers [1960].

Hacking I. (1984). Winner take less. *New York Review of Books, 31*(11), pp. x-x.

Held V. (Ed.) (1995). *Justice and Care: Essential Readings in Feminist Ethics*. Boulder: Westview Press.

Kittay E. F. & Feder E. K. (Ed.) (2002). *The Subject of Care. Feminist Perspectives on Dependency*. New York: Rowman and Littlefield.

Kohlberg L. (1981). *The Philosophy of Moral Development*. San Francisco: Harper and Row.

Larrabee M. J. (Ed.). (1993). *An Ethic of Care. Feminist and interdisciplinary perspectives*. New York: Routledge.

Laugier S. (1999). *Du réel à l'ordinaire. Quelle philosophie du langage aujourd'hui ?* Paris: Vrin.

Laugier S. (2004). *Une autre pensée politique américaine: La démocratie radicale d'Emerson à Stanley Cavell*. Paris: Michel Houdiard.

Laugier S. (2005). To Rethink the Ordinary: Austin After Cavell. In Goodman R. B. (Ed.), *Contending With Stanley Cavell* (pp. 82-99). Oxford: Oxford University Press.

Laugier S. (Ed.). (2006). *Ethique, littérature, vie humaine*. Paris: Presses universitaires de France.

Laugier S. (2006). Wittgenstein and Cavell: Anthropology, Skepticism and Politics. In Norris A. (Ed.), *The Claim to Community: Essays on Stanley Cavell and Political Philosophy* (pp. 19-37). Stanford: Stanford University Press.

Laugier S. (2007b). The myth of the outer: Wittgenstein's redefinition of subjectivity. In Moyal-Sharrock D. (Ed.), *Perspicuous Presentations, Essays on Wittgenstein's Philosophy of Psychology* (pp. 151-173). Basingstoke: Palgrave Macmillan.

Laugier S. (2009). *Wittgenstein, Les sens de l'usage*. Paris: Vrin.

Laugier S. (2010). *Wittgenstein, Le mythe de l'inexpressivité*. Paris: Vrin.

Laugier S. (2010, April 21). *Politique du care contre société du soin*. https://blogs.mediapart.fr/sandra-laugier/blog/210410/politique-du-care-contre-societe-du-soin

Laugier S. (2010, June 20). *Yes We Care!* https://blogs.mediapart.fr/sandra-laugier/blog/200610/yes-we-care

Laugier S. (2011). Matter and Mind: Cavell's (Concept of) Importance. *MLN, 126*(5), pp. 994-1003.

Laugier S. & Ginsburg D. (2011). Introduction to the French edition of *Must We Mean What We Say? Critical Inquiry, 37*(4), pp. 627-651.

Laugier S. (2012). *Tous vulnérables? Le care, les animaux, l'environnement.* Paris: Payot.
Laugier S. (2013a). *Why We Need Ordinary Language Philosophy*, trans. Ginsburg D. Chicago: Chicago University Press.
Laugier S. (2013b). Attention to Ordinary Others: Care, Vulnerability, and Human Security. *Iride*, *3*, pp. 507-526.
Laugier S. (2013c). The Will to See: Ethics and Moral Perception of Sense, trans. Chalier J., *Graduate Faculty Philosophy Journal*, *34*(2), pp. 263-281.
Laugier S. (2015) The Ethics of Care as a Politics of the Ordinary, *New Literary History*, 46, 2015, p. 217-240.
Laugier S. (2016a) Care, the Ordinary, Forms of Life, *Iride. Filosofia e discussione pubblica*, n° 1/2016, p. 109-121.
Laugier S. (2016b) Politics of Vulnerability and Responsibility for Ordinary Others, *Critical Horizons, A Journal of Philosophy and Social Theory*, Volume 17, 2016 - Issue 2: *The Politics of Vulnerability*.
Laugier S. (2020). Ordinary Realism in Ethics. In Vosman F., Baart A., Hoffman J. (Eds.), *The Ethics of Care, the State of the Art.* Leuven-Paris-Bristol: Peeters, pp. 113-136.
Lovell A. (2013) Aller vers les invisibilisés: Katrina, maladie mentale et care dans des circonstances extraordinaires, in Lovell A., Pandolfo S., Das V. & Laugier S. (Eds.) (2013).
Lovell A., Pandolfo S., Das V. & Laugier S. (Eds.). (2013). *Face aux désastres*. Paris: Ithaque.
Margalit A. (2002). *The Ethics of Memory*. Cambridge: Harvard University Press.
McDowell J. (1994). *Mind and World.* Cambridge: Harvard University Press.
Mill J. S. (1859). *On Liberty*. Gertrude Himmelfarb G. (Ed.). London: Penguin.
Moi T. (2005). *Sex, Gender, and the Body: The Student Edition of What Is a Woman?* Oxford: Oxford University Press.
Molinier P. et al. (2009). *Qu'est-ce que le care?* Paris: Payot.
Murdoch I. (1997). Vision and Choice in Morality. In Murdoch I & Conradi P. J. (Eds.), *Existentialists and Mystics: Writings on Philosophy and Literature*. London: Chatto and Windus.
Noddings N. (1984). *Caring: A Feminine Approach to Ethics and Moral Education.* Berkeley: University of California Press.
Norgaard K. M. (2006). 'We Don't Really Want to Know': Environmental Justice and Socially Organized Denial of Global Warming in Norway. *Organization and Environment* 19(3): pp. 347-470.
Norris A. (Ed.). (2006). *The Claim to Community*. Stanford: Stanford University Press.
Nussbaum M. (1990). *Love's Knowledge, Essays on Philosophy and Literature*. Oxford: Oxford University Press.
Nussbaum M. (2000a). *Women and Human Development: The Capabilities Approach*. Cambridge: Cambridge University Press.
Nussbaum M. (2000b). Women's Capabilities and Social Justice. *Journal of Human Development, 1*(2), pp. 220-247.

Nussbaum M. (2006). *Frontiers of Justice: Disability, Nationality, Species Membership*. Cambridge: Harvard University Press.
Nussbaum M. (2011). *Creating Capabilities: The Human Development Approach*. Oxford: Harvard University Press.
Ogien R. (1999). *Le réalisme moral*. Paris: Presses universitaires de France.
Ogien R. (2004). *La panique morale*. Paris: Grasset.
Ogien A. & Laugier S. (2010). *Pourquoi désobéir en démocratie?* Paris: La Découverte.
Ogien A. & Laugier S. (2014). *Le principe démocratie. Enquêtes sur les nouvelles formes du politique*. Paris: La Découverte.
Onfray M. (2010, June 12). *Martine, Carol, Simone et les autres*. https://www.lemonde.fr/idees/article/2010/06/12/martine-carol-simone-et-les-autres_1371784_3232.html?xtmc=&xtcr=22
Paperman P. & Laugier S. (Eds.). (2005). *Le souci des autres, éthiques et politiques du care*. Paris: Éditions de l'École des hautes études en sciences sociales.
Pateman C. (1988). *The Sexual Contract*. Stanford: Stanford University Press.
Putnam, H. (2004). Ethics without Ontology. Cambridge Mass.: Harvard University Press.
Rawls J. (1971). *A Theory of Justice*. Cambridge: Harvard University Press.
Recanati F. (2004). *Literal Meaning*. Cambridge: Cambridge University Press.
Sen A. (2003). *Human Security Now*. UN Report, Commission on Human Security. New York: Harvard University Press. https://reliefweb.int/sites/reliefweb.int/files/resources/91BAEEDBA50C6907C1256D19006A9353-chs-security-may03.pdf
Sen A. (2009). *The Idea of Justice*. Cambridge: Harvard University Press.
Stocker M. (1976). The Schizophrenia of Modern Ethical Theories. In Crisp R. & Slote M. (Eds.), *Virtue Ethics* (pp. 66-78). Oxford: Oxford University Press.
Taylor C. (1985). Language and Human Nature. In *Human Agency and Language*. Cambridge: Cambridge University Press.
Travis C. (1989). *The Uses of Sense*. Oxford: Oxford University Press.
Travis C. (2001). *Unshadowed Thought: Representation in Thought and Language*. Cambridge: Harvard University Press.
Tronto J. & Fisher B. (1990). Toward a feminist theory of caring. In Abel E. & Nelson M. (Eds.), *Circles of Care* (pp. 36-54). Albany: State University of New York Press.
Tronto J. (1993). *Moral Boundaries. A Political Argument for an Ethic of Care*. New York: Routledge.
Tronto J. (2005). Care as a Work of Citizens: A Modest Proposal. In Friedman M. (Ed.), *Women and Citizenship* (pp. 130-145). Oxford: Oxford University Press.
Tronto J. (2009). *Foreword to the French edition of Moral Boundaries: A Political Argument for the Ethic of Care (Un monde vulnérable), trans. Hervé Maury*. Paris: La Découverte.
Tronto J. (2012). Partiality Based on Relational Responsibilites: Another Approach on Global Ethics. *Ethics and Social Welfare*, 6 (3), pp. 303-316.
Wittgenstein L. (1921).*Tractatus logico-philosophicus*. London & New York: Routledge & Kegan Paul.

Wittgenstein L. (1923). *Lecture on Ethics*. Zamuner E., Di Lascio E. V. & Levy D. K. (Eds.). Oxford: Blackwell.
Wittgenstein L. (1948). *Remarks on the Philosophy of Psychology, Vol. 2*. von Wright G. H., Nyman H. & Luckhardt C. G. (Eds.). Chicago: University Press of Chicago.
Wittgenstein L. (1953). *Philosophical Investigations, transl. Anscombe* G. E. M. Oxford: Blackwell.
Wittgenstein L. (1958). *The Blue and Brown Books*. Oxford: Blackwell.
Wittgenstein L. (1971). *ProtoTractatus—An Early Version of Tractatus Logico-Philosophicus*, 1971, B. F. McGuinness, T. Nyberg, G. H. von Wright (Eds.), D. F. Pears and B. F. McGuinness (trans.). Ithaca: Cornell University Press.
Zerilli L. (2005). *Feminism and the Abyss of Freedom*. Stanford: Stanford University Press.
Zerilli L. (2009). Toward a Feminist Theory of Judgment. *Signs*, 34(2), pp. 295-317.

Ethics of Care

1. C. Leget, C. Gastmans, M. Verkerk (Eds.), *Care, Compassion and Recognition. An Ethical Discussion*, 2011, IV-250 p.
2. A. van Heijst, *Professional Loving Care. An Ethical View of the Healthcare Sector*, 2011, VI-212 p.
3. G. Olthuis, H. Kohlen, J. Heier (Eds.), *Moral Boundaries Redrawn. The Significance of Joan Tronto's Argument for Political Theory, Professional Ethics, and Care as Practice*, 2014, IV-232 p.
4. I. van Nistelrooij, *Sacrifice. A Care-Ethical Reappraisal of Sacrifice and Self-Sacrifice*, 2015, X-302 p.
5. R. J. Lynch, *Care: An Analysis*, 2016, X-305 p.
6. S. Bourgault, E. Pulcini (Eds.), *Emotions and Care: Interdisciplinary Perspectives*, 2018, VI-262 p.
7. F. Brugère, *Care Ethics*, 2019, VI-101 p.
8. F. Vosman, A. Baart, J. Hoffman (Eds.), *The Ethics of Care: The State of the Art*, 2020, VIII-317 p.
9. F. Vosman, P. Nortvedt (Eds.), *Care Ethics and Phenomenology: a Contested Kinship*, 2020, VIII-226 p.
10. S. Bourgault, F. Vosman (Eds.), *Care Ethics in yet a Different Voice: Francophone Contributions*, 2020, VI-335 p.

PRINTED ON PERMANENT PAPER • IMPRIME SUR PAPIER PERMANENT • GEDRUKT OP DUURZAAM PAPIER - ISO 9706
N.V. PEETERS S.A., WAROTSTRAAT 50, B-3020 HERENT